God's Redneck Social Justice Warrior

God's Redneck Social Warrior

A Bible Study in Amos

Charles Rushing

XULON PRESS

Xulon Press Elite
2301 Lucien Way #415
Maitland, FL 32751
407.339.4217
www.xulonpress.com

© 2022 by Charles Rushing

All rights reserved solely by the author. The author guarantees all contents are original and do not infringe upon the legal rights of any other person or work. No part of this book may be reproduced in any form without the permission of the author.

Due to the changing nature of the Internet, if there are any web addresses, links, or URLs included in this manuscript, these may have been altered and may no longer be accessible. The views and opinions shared in this book belong solely to the author and do not necessarily reflect those of the publisher. The publisher therefore disclaims responsibility for the views or opinions expressed within the work.

Unless otherwise indicated, Scripture quotations taken from the Holy Bible, New International Version (NIV). Copyright © 1973, 1978, 1984, by International Bible Society. Used by permission of Zondervan. All rights reserved.

Unless otherwise indicated, Scripture quotations taken from the New American Standard Bible (NASB). Copyright © 1960, 1962, 1963, 1968, 1971, 1972, 1973, 1975, 1977, by The Lockman Foundation. Used by permission. All rights reserved.

Unless otherwise indicated, Scripture quotations taken from the New King James Version (NKJV). Copyright © 1982 by Thomas Nelson, Inc. Used by permission. All rights reserved.

Unless otherwise indicated, Scripture quotations taken from the English Standard Version (ESV). Copyright © 2000, 2001 by Crossway Bibles, a publishing ministry of Good News Publishers. Used by permission. All rights reserved.

Paperback ISBN-13: 978-1-6628-5438-5
Ebook ISBN-13: 978-1-6628-5439-2

To Diana, my wife, muse, encourager, greatest fan and lover for 53 years.

Contents

Introduction ix

Chapter One. The Redneck Trolls North 1

Chapter Two. Four Quarts in a Three-quart Bucket 13

Chapter Three. The Circling Lion 25

Chapter Four. Prey Not Pray. 35

Chapter Five. Spiritual Mad Cow Disease 45

Chapter Six. The Walking Dead. 55

Chapter Seven. Let Justice Roll Down Like Water. 65

Chapter Eight. Smug Snug Humbugs 75

Chapter Nine. Time to Measure Up. 85

Chapter Ten. Redneck Go Home. 93

Chapter Eleven. The Time is Ripe 103

Chapter Twelve. A Way Forward 113

Introduction

When my wife, Diana, and I left our ministry in the Tibetan regions of China to retire at home in the United States, we were shocked at the social divisiveness at home. Anyone who has traveled abroad knows that the US is probably the most tolerant and least racist nation on the planet. Yet somehow the prophets of the "woke". and anti-racist religions has converted much of our shallow thinking public and politicians. I was taught as child that the United States was a melting pot of races, religions, and ideas. In reality it was more like a tossed salad. I never dreamed there would be groups trying to pull the pieces of the salad apart and separate them with bitter vinegar.

The church of Jesus Christ anxiously awaits the moment in Revelations where people of every tribe, nation, and language bows before our Savior. Still today Christianity is also a tossed salad. I can enter any community and find not only separate denominations but Korean churches, black churches, white churches, Spanish churches, and even a cowboy church. Yet, as a fellow believer, I can enter anyone of those congregations and find love and fellowship. That is not the case in wokeism or anti-racism. They have no answer or savior. Therefore, I believe the church needs to dust off the minor prophets and teach how God wants to handle justice and racism.

I wrote this book with the intent of making a difficult to comprehend piece of Scripture digestible to the average Bible reader. Forty years of pastoring demonstrated the need to provide something between a

Bible commentary and a Bible study pamphlet to assist the average reader and seeker of biblical knowledge.

In attempting this concept, I have chosen words in my title that will raise the neck hair on both sides of the political spectrum. To you on the left, I use the term *redneck* in its original meaning as an agricultural worker. Yes, I know the shock value of that designation with the term *social justice* seem incongruous, yet that was my intent. To you on the right, I do know the origin of the Trojan horse term *social justice* from Marxist theology. Yet once again I say I am trying to communicate to the average reader, and the term *social justice* has taken a societal definition that portrays the meaning of Amos's message. To you with a philosophical OCD personality, think of the term *biblical justice* as behind my use of *social justice*.

Rev. Charles Rushing

Chapter One

The Redneck Trolls North

*"We can only know that we know nothing.
And that is the highest degree of human wisdom"*[1]
—Leo Tolstoy

The Message Trumps the Messenger

The COVID-19 pandemic years will go into history as tumultuous times. Not only did the world suffer a pandemic, but we had a North American toilet paper scare, and it became the only time in history where a face mask was the only required clothing at a nudist colony. Yet a worse situation is the polarization of humanity over perceived injustice and inequality. Solomon wrote there is "nothing new under the sun" (see Ecclesiastes 1:9), and all our world's current problems fall into this category. The evangelical preacher pontificates our Bible has all the answers, and it does. The difficulty is many of those *answers* are embedded in language and culture thousands of years distant to digitized western civilization. This book attempts to tackle complex theology, language, and history by slicing them into chewable bites for the average Jack and Jill in the church pew. A look into the life and times of Amos will be a mirror into our modern world, nation, and especially the Christian faith today.

The Cambridge dictionary defines *redneck* as "a poor, white person without education, especially one living in the countryside in the southern U.S., who has prejudiced (= unfair and unreasonable)[2] ideas and beliefs." The term *redneck* was first used in 1839 to describe agricultural workers whose labors exposed their heads to constant sunlight. Although Amos was chronologically distant and half a world away, the modern disparaging term would have gladly been affixed to his name when his original Northern Israel recipients gossiped over his declarations. If we accept the theological precept that God's prophetic words cast a wider net than ancient Israel, then Amos is pointing to a larger public square including today's world.

A study through Amos communicates God's view and cure for social injustice.

Amos, a fig farmer, journeyed from southern Judah with the smell of sheep dung clinging to his sandals to warn of pernicious inequality in his world. He was a God-endued, bombastic, social warrior, decrying injustice to the poor, eight centuries before Christ. With blistering rhetoric, Amos strips the veneer off religious activity and those playing at faith who exploited humanity for personal gain. Our redneck prophet declared in-your-face consequences for social sins practiced by all mankind. Amos confronts racial hatred, slavery, wealth inequality, indignant bullying, judicial injustice, and social prejudice.

A study through Amos communicates God's view and cure for social injustice. Since God does not change, and man is still a sinner, this study is as relevant today as the morning news. Our world lacks no dearth of polarizing issues. Make your own list, but try: required masks, abortion, vaccines, climate change, gay marriage, women preachers, racial inequality, transgendered issues, tax cuts, immigration, police power, gun control, etc. We live in interesting times. How then should a believer respond? Answers are always relevant in the Bible although modern society declines to seek this permanent cure. In this study Amos locks justice and righteousness into how we treat family, neighbors and society. Is fairness in all our finances? Is equality and equity in all relationships?

Even though we in the west are chronologically and geographically far from Amos, our moral, spiritual, and cultural conditions are very similar. We in the western church are far closer to the human conditions God condemned nearly 2700 years in the past than we realize. Therefore, to bring Amos onto today's soil, we must first meet him in his own setting.

The Designed DNA of God Anointed Servants

God's only requirement is that people know him at the personal level. Jesus said, live in me and I will live in you (see John 15:4). God does not share his glory therefore his servants have little to brag about.

> Thus says the LORD: "Let not the wise man boast in his wisdom, let not the mighty man boast in his might, let not the rich man boast in his riches, but let him who boasts boast in this, that he understands and knows me, that I am the LORD who practices steadfast love, justice, and righteousness in the earth. For in these things I delight, declares the LORD." Jeremiah 9:23–24 (ESV)

To grasp the message of Amos, we must always start where the Bible starts. No matter how uncomfortable, unappealing, and unappetizing it may be to the spiritual diet of modern man, we must start where the Bible starts.

Jeremiah's words remind believers that our divine personal gifts are stuffed into cheap clay pots as the Apostle Paul claimed. Sometimes these precious abilities are hidden from secular eyes.

In January 2007, Joshua Bell, one of the world's greatest violin virtuosos donned a T-shirt and a baseball cap and played his $3.5 million Stradivarius in the subway station at L'Enfant Plaza in Washington, DC. For an approximate hour, Bell played some of the most beautiful and difficult violin solos ever written. Over a thousand commuters passed the young man with only one individual recognizing what they were hearing. It makes one wonder if the public can recognize true greatness when it's in humble wrappings.

To grasp the message of Amos, we must always start where the Bible starts. No matter how uncomfortable, unappealing, and unappetizing it may be to the spiritual diet of modern man, we must start where the Bible starts. The book of Amos hinges on two points of Christian theology. First is the nature of God. Our Judeo-Christian God is sovereign, holy, and merciful. It appears our innate tendency as modern Christians is to gravitate to Jesus, the second person of the Trinity. I think this is because of His example of love, kindness, and forgiveness. Yet, if we acknowledge with intellectual honesty, reality demands the believer must confess the mirror image of mercy which is wrath. Without the wrath of God, there is no need for mercy and forgiveness. The wrath of God is not some uncontrollable emotional outburst. We equate wrath or anger from a human perspective. God is absolutely pure. God is absolutely holy. Therefore, God cannot tolerate things that are impure and unholy.

> "For the wrath of God is revealed from heaven against all ungodliness and unrighteousness of men, who by their unrighteousness suppress the truth. For what can be known about God is plain to them, because God has shown it to them. For his invisible attributes, namely, his eternal power and divine nature, have been clearly

perceived, ever since the creation of the world, in the things that have been made. So, they are without excuse. For although they knew God, they did not honor him as God or give thanks to him, but they became futile in their thinking, and their foolish hearts were darkened." (Romans 1:18–21 ESV)

Paul implied in Romans that "The wrath of God" is revealed against "ungodliness and unrighteousness of men, who by their unrighteousness suppress the truth." Generally, men and women today who use the word *G-o-d* do not know what they're saying. God for them is some cosmic principle. God is the earth; God is this; God is that; The ignorant slot God into whatever pigeon-hole assigned. Therefore, embracing of the name *God*, they are nevertheless godless. Again, according to Paul, it is godlessness which evolves to wickedness or unrighteousness.

Our society fails to accept the link between godlessness and wickedness. The United States has thrown billions and billions of dollars after the symptoms while at the same time refusing to acknowledge the disease. Washington conceives myriad programs—political programs, social programs, educational programs, financial programs—yet displays their total unwillingness to recognize the disease is godlessness. For example, every sensible man and woman in America knows if we would live with one wife in absolute purity and prior to marriage live in absolute purity, we would eliminate all STDs. But since woke society cannot say to people, "You're not allowed to sleep with your girlfriend" or "Homosexuality is wrong, and it is deviant behavior," we are left not addressing the disease but addressing the symptoms. Therefore, culture is passing godless wickedness down to our children and children's children setting society up for judgment

The book of Amos stresses that the Doctrine of Man assumes men and women are created in God's image, therefore must all be respected economically, socially, and physically. God's image is not degraded by race, religion, politics, or geography. This alone makes Amos a social warrior by definition.

Our second theological hinge is in the fact men and women were created in the image of God and lost our innocence in the garden of Eden. This Christian precept is insidiously attacked. The Doctrine of Man is 180 degrees off current social constructs. Today the simple question, "are you male or female," can cause a riot on the college campus. If society can convince itself men and women are simply an evolving animal, then all behavior becomes barnyard activity. Under this scenario, only those who hold power, control the ethics of the barnyard. The treatment of human being become subject to the philosophy of the survival of the fittest. This kind of thinking, which permeates our modern world, is in direct violation of the Bible and our Doctrine of Man. (It is also Christian doctrine that God loves all sinners, but I sinfully enjoy knowing that all woke LBGTQWXYZ sexual libertines still purchase their T-shirts in male and female sizes.)

The book of Amos stresses that the Doctrine of Man assumes men and women are created in God's image, therefore must all be respected economically, socially, and physically. God's image is not degraded by race, religion, politics or geography. This alone makes Amos a social warrior by definition.

In order to bridge time and space, we will need to first discover the original linguistic, cultural, and historical context. The minor prophets are written without innate historical narrative and demand some biblical research to be fully enjoy and understood. This difficulty may be why they are so ignored from our modern Christian pulpits. Because these prophets require a huge background level of Hebrew scriptures and history. I plan to put these concepts on a lower shelf for our modern church attenders.

In obtaining a university education, every student is required to take elective courses outside of their major field of study. I choose to take courses in photography and journalism. I remember learning the "Five Ws" (Who? When? Where? What? Why?). For good journalistic writing these Ws must have prominence in the first paragraph of any news story. The book of Amos provides such information in the first two verses. Like a good news story, the rest of the book simply expands these five.

The Fig Picking Prophet

Amos humbly opens his book answering the who, what, where and when questions.

> The words of Amos, who was among the shepherds of Tekoa, which he saw concerning Israel in the days of Uzziah king of Judah and in the days of Jeroboam the son of Joash, king of Israel, two years before the earthquake. (Amos 1:1 ESV)

In general, a resume of "I'm a back woods shepherd" would not qualify one to take the role of a prophet. I seriously doubt whether Jesus or any of his twelve apostles could survive the expectations of a modern evangelical church pastoral search committees. Do churches value education and experience above the call and empowerment of God? In our current age, I surely hope those criteria are reversed, but I am not convinced.

Isaiah 66:2 says:

> "But this is the one to whom I will look: he who is humble and contrite in spirit and trembles at my word."

The credentials of Amos should give every Christian pause about who fills our evangelical pulpits. I'm not disparaging training and education, but Holy Spirit enduements should be the first priority. God's message is always more significant than the messenger. In an age where the word *selfie* has been added to the dictionary, maybe more "humble and contrite in spirit" would change the course of a culture hell-bent on driving off a cliff. Preaching requires the minister to negotiate the two worlds of God's truth and the daily soil we inhabit in order to make twenty-first century applications from thousand-year-old books. That job is easier with experience and education, but the primary requirement is the sure call of our Creator. Such a man was Amos. What kind of man was our social warrior? A simple shepherd from an agricultural community on edge of the dry regions of Judah, the southern kingdom—"The words of Amos, who was among the shepherds of Tekoa."

Amos may or may not have been a simple shepherd. Of the numerous Old Testament shepherd references, the Hebrew term used here occurs only one other time in 2 Kings 3:4, where it refers to Mesha, king of Moab. Shepherd king Mesha was able to supply Israel with 100,000 lambs and 100,000 rams. A guy capable of shipping 200k sheep is a bit more important than the common shepherd on a Judean hillside. Bible commentators are split over the actual economic and societal influence he wielded in his time. Was Amos a pillar of agricultural business or a country bumkin, Amos' pedigree gets even more confusing when he responds to a challenge by Bethel's High priest, Amaziah, in in chapter 7.

The message has priority over the preacher.

> Then Amos answered and said to Amaziah, "I was no prophet, nor a prophet's son, but I was a herdsman and a dresser of sycamore figs. But the LORD took me

from following the flock, and the LORD said to me, 'Go, prophesy to my people Israel.' Now therefore hear the word of the LORD. (Amos 7:14–16 ESV)

Here the word for *herdsman* indicates larger animals than just sheep, possibly cattle and goats in large numbers. Since all we know about Amos is given in the book, it appears our prophet took pains to emphasize his enormous lack of earthly merit. He courageously states his credentials are only in God's calling to preach. Why? The message has priority over the preacher.

The Word of God has priority over the man. Quite boldly he states, "hear the word of the Lord," immediately after staking the spiritual high ground away from Israel's fully trained and kingly authorized high priest.

The farming village of Tekoa is about five miles south and east of Bethlehem. It is just a short walk to the shepherds' field in the advent announcement. Tekoa's location is on the edge of arable farming land and yielded a very hard existence on the boarder of the Negev wilderness (see 2 Chronicles 20:20). When my wife Diana and I walked that area a few years back, I told her that if Darwinian evolution is true, Judean sheep would have evolved two legs, on one side, longer than the other side. With tongue in cheek, natural selection needed such a mutation to walk those constant hill and valleys. It is hard country, and I also wondered if the Hebrews taught sheep to eat rocks.

A Time of Prosperity and Wealth

The rest of verse one allows us to date Amos's ministry fairly accurately.

Which he saw concerning Israel in the days of Uzziah king of Judah and in the days of Jeroboam the son of

Joash, king of Israel, two years before the earthquake. (Amos 1:1 ESV)

After the reign of Solomon, the people of God split into two kingdoms (see 1 Kings 12–14). The Northern Kingdom of ten tribes assumed the name *Israel* for their nation. This event was about 150 years before Amos appeared. Jeroboam I, their founding king, set up golden calf idols in the towns of Bethel and Dan. He syncretized the Hebrew religion for political gain in order to turn the people away from worship at Solomon's temple in Jerusalem. The Southern Kingdom was named *Judah*, whose kings came from the line of David as God had promised.

The designated monarchs provide a range of time for his prophetic mission. Uzziah, king of Judah, reigned fifty-two years in a stable and prosperous county. The king of Israel had reigned over forty years. Both kings were able to expand their borders until the two kingdoms ruled the same territory that made Solomon wealthy. These two kings had ruled for most of the first half of the eighth century BC. Together they had prospered Israel and Judah similar to the wealth and military might of Solomon. The people believed they were genuinely blessed by God because they were the "chosen people."

The earthquake cited in Amos 1:1 may be the same as that attested by excavations at Hazor dating to approximately 760 BC. Since Amos claimed not to be a professional prophet, he ministered in a short span of time rather than stretching over several decades.

Although sometimes tenuous, there is much to be learned reading between the lines. Obviously, the book was compiled after the earthquake. Since the earthquake is in the date formula, it must have been a substantial event, because three centuries later the memory still hurts (see Zechariah 14:5). Predicting the earthquake in chapters eight and nine cemented Amos credentials as a true prophet (see Deuteronomy 18:22) despite his own professional denials. Also, the fortunes of Israel and Judea were subject to the variable military strength of their stronger neighbors. During the reigns of Uzziah and Jeroboam, Syria was struggling against Assyria, and Egypt had other problems. This let these two kings expand their boarders to match the great kingdom of Solomon, and trade flourished. Both kingdoms' average citizens felt secure, complacent, and wealthy.

> "The LORD roars from Zion and utters his voice from Jerusalem; the pastures of the shepherds mourn, and the top of Carmel withers." (Amos 1:2 ESV)

I'm a Vietnam War combat veteran and stood my ground during face-to-face military fire fights. As a hunter I've held my rifle still and steady in front of a charging grizzly bear and bull moose. Yet through all that, the closest I've come to soiling my knickers was hearing, and not seeing, a male lion roar in tall grass. That is a sound no creature can hear without the fear of impending doom. This is the image Amos uses to open his oracles. Amos lived his life as a shepherd. I imagine, to a shepherd at pasture, the most terrifying sound was the roar of the lion. When Amos wanted to sanction the power of God's word, he likened it to the lion's roar. That is a sound that cannot be ignored. The roar is actually felt as well as heard.

Final Thoughts

I heard a pastor once speak about "spare tire Christians." These are the folks who only run to Jesus when the wheels go flat. If things are going well, they're spiritually tepid, catching fire for the Lord only when things turn bad. Israel and Judah were economically and militarily stable. As is all society, there are always the wealthy and the poor. Still God gave his people Israel laws in order to honor and provide for the poor. The wealthy Hebrews had ignored the Word of God to profit off the poverty of their brothers and sisters. The world will hear a roar out of Judah when our patient God loses His patience. We all must love people and use things instead of loving things and using people. When a society takes God out of human relations, it is like removing your heart and yet expecting life to function normally.

Application

1. Read the biblical qualifications for Christian leadership (1 Timothy 3:113. Titus 1:5–9).

    a.) How would you balance these with a good theological education?

    b.) D. L. Moody was a shoe salesman; A. W. Tozer had a third-grade education. Based on those qualifications, would your church consider either of them for a pastor?

2. Discuss the meaning of Micah 6:8 in relation to church leadership.

3. Compare the call of Amos (7:14) with that of Isaiah (Isaiah 6:1).

Chapter Two

Four Quarts in a Three-Quart Bucket

*"The idea that some lives matter less
is the root of all that is wrong with the world."*
—Paul Farmer[3]

Events in the year 2020 savaged the border city of Tijuana, racking up almost 2,000 murders, earning the label of having the highest murder rate per capita of any city in Mexico.[4] The cartels along the US/Mexico border are responsible for thousands of brutal murders, many with unfathomable atrocities to men, women, and children. No amount of drug traffic can account for the brutality and sheer number of murders. The vicious treatment of human beings' shocks even the most callous first responders. The Bible teaches a moral conscience is part and parcel of the image of God created and embedded into all of mankind. When God's image is diluted, polluted, and hardened, we hasten the silencing of a voice of conscience. The cry of the innocents become muted in hardened hearts.

At one time I had identified myself as a university-trained atheist, yet I struggled with the existence of evil. If evil existed, then an ultimate good must exist simply by definition. This problem is devastating to true atheism. How can there be evil without a good God? Where did mankind get our moral compass to judge good and evil? The image of God, in mankind, produces the human concept of right and wrong and transcends all cultures and religions. The human conscience of good and evil has not been eradicated but has accepted corruption through the fall in the garden of Eden. All humanity is corrupted, but the Bible insists the common grace of our Creator God is extended to all of creation. Still, theology insists the laws of God are written into every human heart (see Romans 2:15). The Bible makes everyone subject to judgment which is a holistic way of inspecting this section of the book of Amos.

The accusation formula is a pattern: "For three transgressions . . . and for four." Consider this phrasing; this Hebrew idiom means the cup overflowed or "I've had enough."

Granddad once blurted "I'm madder than a mule chewing a hornet's nest!" The emphatic southern idiom infers how God feels about the nations surrounding Israel. God slams each nation because of the sin of inhumanity to their fellow men. The overall meaning of Amos's rhetoric screams, "My patience is exhausted now comes judgment." Seven times the messenger's formula begins with, "Thus says Yahweh." The Bible reader should always note when the Lord's name is capitalized in their translations. The emphatic announcement punches out the truth, insisting Amos's proclamation is true prophecy from God himself.

The accusation formula is a pattern: "For three transgressions . . . and for four." Consider this phrasing; this Hebrew idiom means the cup overflowed or "I've had enough". The best modern cliché would paraphrase as "the straw that broke the camel's back." We next read the specific accusation and then an irrevocable judgment of fire. Fire is a widely recognized metaphor for divine judgment throughout biblical literature.

An examination of these seven national sins indicates our modern world is also flirting with God's judgment. The seven nations surrounding Israel represent all of mankind. These nations include both those with revelation, the Bible, and those without Scripture. These verses emphasize all humanity is God's creation and subject to his providence, judgment, and mercy.

Israel's neighbor's atrocities are subject to the Lord's authority and their wicked deeds are outrages against his rule. Gentile neighbors were held responsible for standards of human treatment of one another, not just damage done to Israel; Judah (see Amos 2:4–5), on the other hand, deserved judgment in terms of its response to Yahweh's law. They had the advantage of special revelation from Yahweh Himself. This grouping of both spiritual groups, those in and those out of a divine relationship, condemns all humanity.

Our journey through the first six nations demonstrates the overarching sin of corrupting the image of God in mankind. Judah is also condemned for debasing God's Word.

The Roaring Lion Circles His Prey

Damascus

> Thus says the LORD: "For three transgressions of Damascus, and for four, I will not revoke the punishment, because they have threshed Gilead with threshing sledges of iron." (Amos 1:3–5 ESV)

The tour of mortal disgrace starts in the Aramean hub of Damascus which would be modern Syria. This regional political power could threaten Israel security and affluence. Gilead set east of the Jordan River and north of the Dead Sea (see Joshua 18:7) and enjoyed its rich woodlands (see Jeremiah 22:6; 50:19; Zechariah 10:10) and fertile grazing land. Threshing sledges imply extreme cruelty in the treatment of those who opposed Damascus. Amos echoes the reports of the brutality when the Syrian kings had annihilated the troops of Jehu's son, Jehoahaz:

For the king of Syria had destroyed them and made them like the dust at threshing. (2 Kings 13:7 ESV)

Philistine cities

> Thus says the LORD: "For three transgressions of Gaza, and for four, I will not revoke the punishment, because they carried into exile a whole people to deliver them up to Edom. ...." (Amos 1:6-8)

Damascus is treating human beings like objects no more significant than grain. Because of this, their punishment will be like fire burning them up.

Four cities hailed before the judgment bench: Gaza, mightiest, southernmost; Ashdod, thirty-three kilometers north of Gaza, also about five kilometers inland and on a latitude just south of Jerusalem; Ashkelon, about halfway between the first two cities and directly on the coast, and Ekron, the northernmost city about twenty kilometers inland and less than ten kilometers from Judah's border. Gath is not mentioned.

The act of rebellion described is slave-trading, probably a purely commercial transaction in which the Philistines raided the neighbor towns of Judah and Israel and sold their prisoners to Edom. Whether the Edomites used the slaves to man their ports and mines or sold them to other nations is not mentioned. Neither does Amos state where the Philistines got their prisoners. His emphasis seems to be solely on the outrageous inhumanity of their act. Slavery is a perennial problem and still is not eradicated in our time. According to the Walk Free Foundation, Great Britain is home to an estimated 136,000 modern slaves.[5] In 2017, British authorities handled over 2000 exploitation cases, most as children forced to work on illegal cannabis farms.[6] As I write this, the US/Mexican border is porous enough to offer drug cartels incentive enough to coyote immigrants encumbered with economic slavery in order to pay their smuggling fees. Humanity has not progressed from Amos's oracles.

Tyre

> Thus says the Lord: "For three transgressions of Tyre, and for four, I will not revoke the punishment, because they delivered up a whole people to Edom, and did not remember the covenant of brotherhood. (Amos 1:9 ESV)

The appalling violations of human decency and honor make our Lion roar.

This speech shifts our attention northward to the Phoenician (Lebanese) coast and its rocky island fortress (see Joel 3:4–6). This follows the oracle against Philistia, because it too involves slave-trading with Edom. The scope and tragedy are underlined in the words "whole people," as though entire settlements were uprooted and peddled to the Edomites. The indictment is amplified by the reference to a broken treaty or literally a "covenant of brotherhood." Tyre's treaty partner, with whom she insincerely played, is not mentioned. The point is another reminder where case specifics are not important to Amos. The appalling violations of human decency and honor make our Lion roar.

In 1 Kings 5:1 and 12 we read the king of Tyre and King Solomon had made a treaty of friendship. But selfishly the people of Tyre had broken their agreement and had sold slaves to their enemy (Edom).

Edom

> Thus says the Lord: "For three transgressions of Edom, and for four, I will not revoke the punishment, because he pursued his brother with the sword and cast off all

> pity, and his anger tore perpetually, and he kept his
> wrath forever. (Amos 1:11 ESV)

Edom has played a villainous role in the two previous speeches. He now comes in for his own indictment. The warfare with his brother confirms the key crime. The brother could, of course, be Israel, since Jacob and Esau, Edom's illustrious ancestor, were brothers (see Genesis 25:19–26). I normally resist the temptation of the pastoral "hoity-toity" practice of pretentiously spewing knowledge of original language. Yet sometimes these tidbits can add color, depth, and understanding to what the Scripture means. The Hebrew verb for "cast off" could mean *spoil*, *corrupt*, or *destroy*, referring to sexual violence or physical harm inflicted on innocent citizens by Edom's soldiers.

Edom apparently took hate to a superpower,
scorching their hardened little hearts, therefore incurring God's wrath.

This hints at over-the-top hate. The word *wrath* in the last line of verse 11 has special significance beyond the simple meaning. In the Hebrew, the word is the subject of the two clauses instead of the object. The punch of this linguistic tidbit is lost in the English translation. Not only does it suit the cultural parallelism and poetry of the original, it stresses the concept where Edom's emotions are totally out of control. Again, this hints at over-the-top hate. Edom apparently took hate to a superpower, scorching their hardened little hearts therefore incurring God's wrath. By whatever rationalization Edom claimed, they buttressed their bitterness until it poisoned the national soul.

> "You shall not hate your brother in your heart, but you
> shall reason frankly with your neighbor, lest you incur
> sin because of him." (Leviticus 19:17 ESV)

Edom's overflowing transgression dwelt hidden in the heart where it is kept smoldering until the outward expression overflows into human cruelty. Where hatred is nourished and not allowed to evaporate, it pollutes whomever it touches. How many modern conflicts between nations have not resulted in atrocities from both sides?

We of the Christian faith must remember our sins are just as stinky in God's nostrils as any enemy we perceive. Those who cannot forgive have forgotten their own position as a guilty sinner. How can they stand before God and ask forgiveness for their transgressions?

Ammonites

> Thus says the LORD: "For three transgressions of the Ammonites, and for four, I will not revoke the punishment, because they have ripped open pregnant women in Gilead, that they might enlarge their border." (Amos 1:13–15 ESV)

Ammon's crime relates directly to their geographical location. In the cycles when Israel displayed power, Ammon's territory was constricted between the Moabites on the south, the Israelites of Gilead on the west, Bashan on the north, and the great desert to the east. Their aspirations for territorial acquisition focused them to pick on the most vulnerable. Even today the evil stalwarts prey on the weak.

The vicious assaults on women, together with the mention of the "sword" (see Amos 7:9, 17; 9:4) as the instrument of terror, destroyed vulnerable future generations for personal gain. The rulers will be earmarked for punishment, this time by exile. Rabbah is to be identified with the modern Amman, capital of Jordan.

Moab

> Thus says the Lord: "For three transgressions of Moab, and for four, I will not revoke the punishment, because he burned to lime the bones of the king of Edom. (Amos 2:1–3 ESV)

Moab is indicted next, perhaps because of kinship with Ammon. (The notorious origin of both is chronicled in Genesis 19:30–38.) The geographical location, just south of Ammon and directly east of the Dead Sea. The act of rebellion—desecration of the bones of Edom's king—presupposes some sharp conflict between the brother states.

The crime itself violated the mores of the ancient world which called for respect for the corpse of a royal enemy. In. 2 Kings 9:34, Jehu ordered a decent burial even for Jezebel. The act of burning a body demonstrated an extreme form of criminal punishment (see Genesis38:24; Leviticus 20:14; 21:9) designed to purge completely, the land of its wickedness. The fiery judgment here (see Amos 1:2) is particularly appropriate where the punishment precisely fits the crime. Kerioth may have been singled out for destruction because it housed a shrine for the Moabite deity, Chemosh. Even in Edom, the persistent enemy of Israel and Judah, God would not sanction any disrespect towards the body of a dead person, royal or commoner. We are all in God's image, believer and pagan alike. Created in the image of God, the human body deserves respect even after death.

Judah

> Thus says the Lord: "For three transgressions of Judah, and for four, I will not revoke the punishment, because they have rejected the law of the Lord, and have not kept his statutes, but their lies have led them astray, those after which their fathers walked. So I will send a

fire upon Judah, and it shall devour the strongholds of Jerusalem." (Amos 2:4–5) ESV)

The three to four pattern assumes a list of known crimes of which the final and scale-tipping one is listed. What Amos indicates by this kind of argument is that punishment is more than merited.

In the flow of the judgment speeches, Judah's turn has come. The homeland of Amos is not spared in condemnation. This speech marks a sharp transition from the previous six: though the form remains constant, the content of the indictment has changed markedly. Neither international treaty-breaking or outrageously inhumane conduct are liable, but failure to keep God's laws, especially the laws calling for exclusive worship of God. This crime, like all the others, maligned Yahweh. Yet this crime exclusively belonged to the covenant people. Those who have God's law are more responsible for transgression than those without Scripture. Amos hinted at a historic pattern of rebellion endemic to Hebrews just as there had been a historic salvation pattern by which God in love sought to keep them loyal to His covenant. Amos's theme verse (1:2) hinted of Judah's and Jerusalem's vulnerability: the roaring Lion resonated in their midst.

Final Thoughts

The three to four pattern assumes a list of known crimes of which the final and scale-tipping one is listed. What Amos indicates by this kind of argument is that punishment is more than merited. Yahweh is thoroughly righteous in sending the judgment. Notice the biblical number of seven nations surrounding Israel is the number identified with completeness. Among those seven are nations with no divine revelation, nations with partial revelation and even Judah with God-given revelation and law. All these peoples represent mankind since all are created in the image of God. These crimes, tipping the scale, are atrocities against God's divine image given to humans. It is Yahweh personally who sends the fire, cuts off the corrupt leaders, and leads the peoples into exile, demonstrating righteous concerns for international politics and human welfare.

Although Amos's prophecy designated the Northern Nation of Israel, we should remember he dwelt in the Southern Kingdom, whose destruction he portended in verses 4–5. Surely, then, his heart must have been heavy as he uttered these words about his beloved city of Jerusalem. 1 Peter 4:17 tells us judgment begins "with the household [family] of God" (ESV). When we visualize the current condition of the world Church, we need to pause and ask forgiveness.

Application

1. In Jesus's Parable of the Tenants (Mark 12:1–12) we are told about the tenants who refused to give the owner of the vineyard his rightful share of the fruit. Notice how their disobedience to the servants eventually led to the murder of the owner's son. What does this parable tell us about the way people react to the prophets and Jesus Christ?

2. Read 1 John 4:20 and James 1:27

    a.) Are fellow Christians, only our brothers and sisters—or also sinners to be tolerated?

    b.) How do we treat and view non-believers.

3. What are some of the consequences for those who do "not obey the gospel of God" (see 1 Peter 4:17; Matthew 25:31–46; 2 Thessalonians 1:8–9)?

Chapter Three

The Circling Lion

*"I like your Christ, I do not like your Christians.
Your Christians are so unlike your Christ."*[7]
—Mahatma Gandhi

When I ponder the spiritual condition of our modern world, I am amazed knowing even the pagan religions recognize there are moral and ethical absolutes in creation. Although Amos's original listeners would have considered God's prophetic condemnation complete at the seven surrounding nations, his oracle continues to illuminate a mirror image reflecting Israel's sins. If God expects the pagans to adhere to human dignity, what does He expect from His "chosen people." Our redneck prophet bullseyes the center object of his prophecy. This passage portrays a lion circling his prey, the nation of Israel. He snared the Northern Kingdom into a got-you moment.

When I first read Amos chapter two, I immediately thought about Mahatma Gandhi's famous saying about Christians not following Christ. Every Christian pastor has heard the secular comment, "the church is full of hypocrites". I would usually respond by saying, "there is always room for one more," but my glib comment ignores the root reason of the secular complaint. Unbelievers feel justified when the Christians are spotted failing in their faith. Tabloids jubilantly run articles about preachers discovered red-handed in the offering or stumbling into moral failure. Social media enjoys pouring salt into these episodes. The pagans gloat over the wounds Christ suffers when his followers profane his teachings. This type of behavior echoes the point behind the message of our redneck preacher in Amos chapter two. Whenever God and His Word are ignored, morality is diluted to nothing. The situation echoes the old saying, "If you stand for nothing, you will fall for anything." Judah and Israel had abandoned their relationship with God. Abandoning God always leads to moral and ethical collapse because like nature, culture also abhors a vacuum. Unfortunately, this Hebrew's vacuum sucked up the six pagan cultures surrounding them. To get the full impact of Amos's Hebrew poetry, we should peruse chapter 2:6–12 as a unit. By this method we observe the entire forest before looking at the trees, to paraphrase an idiom.

Notice the crowning sin of these examples is reducing human life to chattel.

> Thus says the LORD: "For three transgressions of Israel, and for four, I will not revoke the punishment, because they sell the righteous for silver, and the needy for a pair of sandals— those who trample the head of the poor into the dust of the earth and turn aside the way of the afflicted; a man and his father go in to the same girl, so that my holy name is profaned; they lay themselves down beside every altar on garments taken in pledge, and in the house of their God they drink the wine of those who have been fined. "Yet it was I who destroyed the Amorite before them, whose height was like the height of the cedars and who was as strong as the oaks; I destroyed his fruit above and his roots beneath. Also, it was I who brought you up out of the land of Egypt and led you forty years in the wilderness,

to possess the land of the Amorite. And I raised up some of your sons for prophets, and some of your young men for Nazirites. Is it not indeed so, O people of Israel?" declares the LORD. "But you made the Nazirites drink wine, and commanded the prophets, saying, 'You shall not prophesy.'" (Amos 2:6–12 ESV)

One Atrocity with Four Tributaries

Notice the crowning sin of these examples is reducing human life to chattel. Exploiting humanity confers the same sins as the surrounding nations. What is reprehensible to God plays out as oppression, misuse, and abuse of helpless people for the profit of the elite. In 1948 the United Nations drafted a Universal Proclamation on Human Rights[8] giving all humanity, regardless of race, religion, or political entity, the inherent rights of life, liberty, and property. This document outlawed slavery, torture, and any behaviors decimating the innate value of human life. Yet today's UN Council on Human Rights lists member nations like China, Cuba, and Islamic nations where slavery and torture are common political practice and process. These are nations where women are still treated as property, denied education or even liberty. In China, dissidents are organ harvested for the black-market trade of human body parts. What happened to the ideals of 1948 UN? The United Nations failed to account for our fundamentally flawed human nature we all inherited from Eden's fall. Amos obvious shows us these conditions are not something new. It is probably easier to comprehend causation of Israel's sins by categorizing their failure into three overall themes: (1) forgetting God's blessings, (2) disparaging God's council, and (3) no future focus.

Notice the similar pattern as the previous nations with a final sin representing the overflow of atrocities. In the verses about Israel, it seems the fourth transgression appears to lists four distinct sins. Why break the previous patterns of only one overflowing transgression?

Amos's poetry lists four examples as a symptom of the larger fourth sin breaking the camel's back. Their foremost sin was forgetting God's reality, and in that vacuum real values of truth, mercy, and justice disappear. They have forgotten His past mercies and simply ignored his teachings as irrelevant. Isaiah 59:14 sums the situation well:

> "Justice is turned back, and righteousness stands far away; for truth has stumbled in the public squares, and righteousness cannot enter." (ESV)

Forgetting the Lord, precedes the sins of injustice, immorality, and idolatry as in the listed examples. When the dominant vice is spiritual amnesia, what follows are major tributaries of depravity and iniquity. The scriptures are not simply for show on the book shelf, but absolutely paramount in the heart. Knowledge of Scripture anticipates a life by scripture. The presence of the law is not the same as obedience to the law. This one lapse cascades into a glut of sin and consequences. A similar problem exists in our world where judges have no judgment and truth blows in the wind. Amos describes a society where ethics are a subject taught and morality is not lived.

Tributary One: Social Injustice and Legal Perversion

> "They sell the righteous for silver, and the needy for a pair of sandals—those who trample the head of the poor into the dust of the earth and turn aside the way of the afflicted." (Amos 2:6 ESV)

I searched the Departments of Justice's web site for the term *corrupt judges*. The computer returned 25,579 articles in their current listings. Most of these dealt with the corruption of bribery. An example would be Judge Mark Ciavarella. He gained the nickname of "Mr. Zero Tolerance" because of harsh juvenile sentences. For example, an 11-year-old got sentenced to two years in a detention center for stealing and driving his mother's car one block. Judge Ciavarella's criminal trial revealed over the years that this corrupt man had earned over one million dollars in kickbacks—all this money from one "for profit" juvenile detention center. Corrupt courts exist beyond the providence of ancient Israel.

Clarity in Hebrew law said the owner owned the person's labor, not the individual.

Our redneck prophet speaks, first of all, about the behavior of Israel's judges: "They sell the righteous for silver, and the needy for a pair of sandals." Honest people who could be trusted to repay eventually were sold for the silver they owed. The desperately poor were enslaved because they could not pay back the insignificant sum, equal to a pair of sandals. The law allowed the Hebrew poor to sell himself (see Leviticus 25:39). But he was not a slave, but rather treated as a hired servant or sojourner; and at the year of jubilee, he became free. Clarity in Hebrew law said the owner owned the person's labor, not the individual. Fast forward to Amos's time and the courts had gone into collusion with the creditors. The judges were denying justice to the oppressed.

The meaning of these verses confirms the poor were being sold for either money or land. The callous treatment against Israel's own people scandalized Amos. Those actions were a rebellion against God's covenant which called for generosity and openhandedness toward the poor (see Deuteronomy 15:7–11). Both the Old and New Testament conclude the poor will always exist. God distresses over the treatment of the poor, not necessarily poverty itself. Even during Israel theocracy where wealth redistributed every fifty years in a Year of Jubilee, it would only take another forty-nine years for economic inequality to raise the gap between haves and have nots. It should be noted God will judge individuals for how they treat the indigent. God may destroy nations, institutions and/or corporations for maligning the poor, but it is the people making those institutions, nations, and corporations who should fear hell fire.

Amos point is a corrupt judicial system financed the pleasures of the wealthy on the back of societies poor. Those in charge had as much concern for the poor as they did for the dirt or gravel they walked upon daily.

Tributary Two: Immorality

If God becomes irrelevant, then his moral laws are considered irrelevant. A people without God will develop other gods, generally made in their own image. I believe only this type of society could invent a new term called a *selfie*.

> "A man and his father go in to the same girl, so that my holy name is profaned." (Amos 2:7 ESV)

Notice in verse seven, the forbidden sexual practice is linked to profaning the name of God. Confusion exists to exactly what linkage is described in the text. In context, the girl involved could be a household slave or servant forced into prostitution by her master and son. To *profane* God's name communicated him as *common* or *ordinary*. Yahweh is holy and exalted. To ignore God's laws and decrees concedes to treat him and his precepts as inconsequential, like ignoring a speed limit if the police are not around. This type of behavior would debase God's unique relationship with Israel.

Yet because of Israel's syncretistic propensity to add the Canaanite worship of Baal, verse seven could also mean the use of temple prostitutes in pagan fertility worship. The economy of the whole area depended on successful agricultural production. In an attempt to achieve agricultural abundance, the Canaanites acted out fertility rites in the temples of their gods. When sex becomes part of worship, immorality will run rampant in society. Either of two interpreted sins are a violation of the Mosaic law, demeaning the treatment of women and God himself.

Tributary Three: Idolatry

> "They lay themselves down beside every altar on garments taken in pledge, and in the house of their God they drink the wine of those who have been fined."(Amos 2:8 ESV)

God's Law placed restrictions on items which could be taken as collateral. Millstones were not to be taken since they were needed for grinding grain and thus were essential to sustaining life (see Deuteronomy 24:6). The cloak of a poor man could not to be kept as a pledge overnight (see Deuteronomy. 24:10–13); a widow's garment could not be taken in pledge at all (see Deuteronomy 24:17). Yet the people openly and flagrantly were lying down at pagan temples with the forbidden garments, going so far in their contempt for the Law as to spread them at the sacrificial feasts by every pagan altar. In addition to this, they used the money extorted from the poor to go on drinking sprees: they had caroused with wine exacted from the people by unjust fines. These people were able to insult God by multiplexing transgressions with wanton abandon.

Results of Multiplexed Transgressions

> "Yet it was I who destroyed the Amorite before them, whose height was like the height of the cedars and who was as strong as the oaks; I destroyed his fruit above and his roots beneath. Also, it was I who brought you up out of the land of Egypt and led you forty years in the wilderness, to possess the land of the Amorite. And I raised up some of your sons for prophets, and some

> of your young men for Nazirites. Is it not indeed so, O people of Israel?" declares the Lord. "But you made the Nazirites drink wine, and commanded the prophets, saying, 'You shall not prophesy.' "Behold, I will press you down in your place, as a cart full of sheaves presses down. Flight shall perish from the swift, and the strong shall not retain his strength, nor shall the mighty save his life; he who handles the bow shall not stand, and he who is swift of foot shall not save himself, nor shall he who rides the horse save his life; and he who is stout of heart among the mighty shall flee away naked in day," declares the Lord. (Amos 2:9–16 ESV)

Notice God reminds them their salvation progressed only through him. He chose them; He defeated their enemies; He gave them their scriptures and guides. The Hebrew people contributed nothing. It should remind Christians the same is true for Christ.

Versus 9 thru 16 is the poetic way of saying, you won't win, and you can't break even. Notice the Scripture uses the first-person singular verb emphasizing they owe all to the Lord. God is essentially saying: "I defeated your enemies; I covenanted with you and led you for forty years in the desert; I gave you land of your own." God also provided them with spiritual examples in the Nazirites and guides with the prophets all to be forgotten and spurned.

These same sins are illustrated in the New Testament. The Lord Jesus Christ wept over Jerusalem because the people killed the prophets and stoned those sent there (see Matthew 23:37), and Paul warned the early church men would continue to "arise and distort the truth in order to draw away disciples after them" (Acts 20:30 NIV).

> *However, with every warning of coming judgment, there is always a call to repentance, whether specifically spoken or, as here, merely implied.*

In verses 13–16 of Amos 2 gives a very vivid description of the punishment which will come upon disobedient Israel. They will be crushed (not merely bruised) "as a cart crush when loaded with grain" (NIV). There will be no escape for the swift runners, the strong, the warriors, the archers, the fleet-footed soldiers, the horsemen, or the bravest warriors. They will go, naked, out of existence on "that day" when the Lord comes in divine judgment upon them. In fact, "that day" did arrive, when Assyria transported Israel away, never to be heard of again.

However, with every warning of coming judgment, there is always a call to repentance, whether specifically spoken or, as here, merely implied. Still today individuals ignore God's warnings. People consistently chase the conventions of the society in which they live, even when the culture contravenes God's Word.

Final Thoughts

The United States of America has lost its own soul. I am a product of a public education, and as a child every morning we recited the pledge of allegiance and the Lord's prayer. I remember my grade school teachers reading from the Bible. What has happened? In "Christianese" we can say America has lost its soul. Apathy and numbness have crept into the halls of power, and something in our collective moral psyche has expired. In Scripture God has promised nations when they will humble themselves, pray, seek his face, and turn from their wicked ways, He would heal the land. It is time for churches to stop playing church and start being the Church. Pastors need to take a lesson from the Civil Rights Movement in the 1960s where pastors were the leaders and politicians followed.

Churches, too, are tempted to adopt practices which ignore the clear teaching of God's Word, but if they yield to national collective apathy, they will soon fall away from the gospel message. Even those strong sound churches where the pure Word of God is faithfully preached can become guilty of merely listening to God's Word, but not doing it (see James 1:23). Sadly, people are moving the goalposts in the Bible to fit in with their lives. I have met people who find good sound reasons for their behavior, but they really assert reasons that sound good. The search for self-satisfaction has become more important than justice and righteousness. The simplest definition of sin is ignoring God.

Application

1. Western democracies are some of the freest and richest nations in the world. Will they always remain so?

2. Read the following Scriptures: Deuteronomy 18:10; Psalms 140:12; 2 Thessalonians 3:6-9. Who should be responsible for assisting the poor? Individuals? Corporations? Governments? When millions of people live in poverty in our rich society, is it their own fault?

3. How is Amos more than a modern social reformist?

4. Read 2 Kings 17:13–21. What were the consequences of Israel and Judah's failure to keep God's commands and honor the covenant He had made with them?

Chapter Four

Prey Not Pray

"Let us try to teach generosity and altruism, because we are born selfish."[8]
—*Atheist Richard Dawkins*

The following warnings were on product labels.

On a curling iron—"for external use only"
On a portable stroller—"Caution: Remove infant before folding for storage"
On packaging for an iron—"Do not iron clothes on body"
On a kid-sized Superman costume—"Wearing this garment does not enable you to fly"
On a hammer—"May be harmful if swallowed"

Common sense should inspire a thoughtful response to every situation. The above warnings must have resulted from actions by consumers who somehow invented unique uses for the product. Corporate lawyers believe warnings would shield their products from lawsuits.

Israel's legal minds were ignoring warning signs outlined in their covenant with God and detailed in Leviticus, Numbers, and Deuteronomy.

No Satisfaction

Haggai 1:5–7 says:

> Now therefore, thus says the LORD of hosts: "Consider your ways! You have sown much, and bring in little; You eat, but do not have enough; You drink, but you are not filled with drink; You clothe yourselves, but no one is warm; And he who earns wages, earns wages to put into a bag with holes." Thus says the LORD of hosts: "Consider your ways!" (NKJV)

When the rock group, the Rolling Stones, sang "I can't get no satisfaction," God proclaims there is a reason for such a sentiment. The Bible consistently announces consequences for abandoning truth and righteousness.

Amos expressed God's outrage against a society insensitive to righteous justice, a culture that materialistically exalted profit over people. America today, like Israel of old, also experiences unequalled prosperity amid poverty. There are great class distinctions in our own society. Unfortunately, the popular political answer is to dole relief instead of providing equal opportunity and dignified employment. Without equal opportunity, society builds a caste system where those with power feed off of the lower castes. The premise of the popular *Hunger Games* books and movies is built upon a caste system.

Our readings demonstrate how God's anger flashes out against those who oppress the indigent. Much Scripture proclaims the poor and humble of the earth are very precious to Him. Men and women concerned with only their personal leisure, profit, and pleasure deeply offend our creator.

> Hear this word that the LORD has spoken against you, O children of Israel, against the whole family which I

brought up from the land of Egypt, saying: "You only have I known of all the families of the earth; therefore, I will punish you for all your iniquities." (Amos 3:1–2 NKJV)

In this message Amos declared Israel would be punished because of her unique relationship with God.

Our cause-and-effect world forms the schema for Amos's poetry in Chapter three. It is always hoped rhetorical questions gain an assumed correct and common-sense response to everything that follows.

The chapter opens with the imperative verb of *hear* which is the Hebrew term *shama*, a compelling prophetic opening signaling an important message will follow. Amos will use this three times to focus on the central message of the book. The major idea behind the whole book is the Hebrew people abandoning their relationship with God. This message resonates from Amos into our time and culture.

Chapter three details that with the privilege of being God's chosen comes responsibility to honor God's law and designs. This precept—abuse of special privilege merits special judgment—becomes the emphasis for the rest of the book. The message addressed initially both to Israel and Judah (vv. 1–2), but then concentrated primarily on the Northern Kingdom. In the opening verse Amos emphasizes God speaking, not man, not society, not politics or agendas. There are times in human history when God speaks. There are times in human history where God transmits something important. It could be a warning or a judgment or even a proclamation of His plans and purposes. But God speaks to His people and to His world, and there's a reason for it. When the Lord of creation speaks, it is expected for people to take notice. He is Lord over both believers and pagans therefore all should hear *shama*.

Common Sense Answers

Newton's third law says for every action there is an opposite reaction, therefore most people realize actions have consequences.

Our cause-and-effect world forms the schema for Amos's poetry in Chapter three. It is always hoped rhetorical questions gain an assumed correct and common-sense response to everything that follows.

A Sunday school teacher queried her young students, "What's furry and eats hazelnuts?" The children searched each other's faces, each one drawing the same conclusion but puzzled how to answer their teacher. Years of experience had taught them how they were expected to show their scriptural knowledge. Finally, one brave young man raised his hand, and the teacher pointed to him. "We know the answer is Jesus," he began, "but it sure sounds like a squirrel to me!"

Our own culture and society have begun to condition responses to situations that are anti-God and anti-Bible. For example, simply look at television programing and commercials pushing homosexual behavior, cohabitation, and fornication.

Seven Questions

> Can two walk together, unless they are agreed? Will a lion roar in the forest, when he has no prey? Will a young lion cry out of his den, if he has caught nothing? Will a bird fall into a snare on the earth, where there is no trap for it? Will a snare spring up from the earth, if it has caught nothing at all? If a trumpet is blown in a city, will not the people be afraid? If there is calamity in a city, will not the LORD have done it? (Amos 3:3–5 NKJV)

Each of the first five questions (vv. 3–5) argues from an observed result to an assumed cause. The result of two people walking together the cause must be an appointment. The expected answer is no. The

Septuagint reads "except they know one another," establishing a relationship between the pedestrians. There is a deeper meaning to this question coming first. Many commentators believe this may point to the covenant between God and Israel, a relationship in extreme danger.

If the result is a lion's roar, the cause must be his prey. So without the hunt there is no roar, no result without the cause. The intent of these questions is not to instruct us in ancient hunting techniques but to set up a series of automatic common sense *no* answers. Amos is the real hunter here. Verse 6 springs the trap. Disaster will strike Israel, and when it does, the Lord Himself will have been responsible.

The Voice of the Prophet

We are living in a generation where a number of people speaking for God declare everything will be well. All is about to get better. Today in many churches that seems to be the dominant message. Sometimes I feel the theology is from the Beatles, "All you need is Love!" Most believers don't know the word *love* is not even mentioned in the first three gospels, and John uses it specifically defined. If we do not immerse ourselves in Scripture, we can sometimes miss God's voice, the real voice. It is a time when the biblical tools for discernment are needed more than ever. Christians need to take these tools and apply them to what we hear being taught in God's name.

Consider what happened in Jeremiah's day: the consensus of official prophets was that everything would be well with God's people. God would defend them from their enemies. God wouldn't use pagans morally far worse than the Hebrews (see Jeremiah 6:14; 8:11) for punishment. Jeremiah stood years virtually alone in warning the nation of the coming judgment. Jeremiah was a voice crying in the wilderness. Who would believe his warnings when the survey of "prophets" proclaimed God would defend His special people? We should expect God's spokespeople to communicate what God is saying, not just what people want to hear. One would also expect not to just follow the trend of other prophets they simply respect. Prophecy is practical. It is the job of the preacher to properly handle God's word. It gives us courage to trust God and look forward to His providence. God never abandons His people. On the surface it may look like things are out of control and no longer His concern. Scripture teaches He keeps His promises and watches over His people.

Prophesy is not a light thing. There is a danger in using the gift to suit an individual's own fancy. In the hands of the wrong people, it can be a very confusing. The people of Israel felt it so very serious that just to claim to speak prophesy falsely and incorrectly meant death. Isaiah and Jeremiah both were hesitant to speak prophecy. It took a divine kick in the pants to respond to the call of God in their lives. It was under such a stringent law that the prophetic utterance claimed so much of the Scripture that came into being. In every book of the Bible there is contained a measure of prophecy. The very heart of God is openly displayed by prophecy.

It took a divine kick in the pants to respond to the call of God in their lives.

Verse seven exhibits God's mercy and love amid the severe consequences of Israel's rejection. Through the prophets, the Lord always revealed His plans in advance. The hearer of the prophetic word must realize certain fulfillment. Since the Lord had made his voice known, like the roar of a lion, Amos has led his hearers through a catechism of common-sense questions to a double conclusion. Yahweh will bring disaster, and Amos has no choice but to announce it.

"Proclaim in the palaces at Ashdod, and in the palaces in the land of Egypt, and say: 'Assemble on the mountains of Samaria; See great tumults in her midst, And the oppressed within her. For they do not know to do right,' Says the Lord, 'Who store up violence and robbery in their palaces.'" (Amos 3:9–10 NKJV)

Prey Not Pray

With God pouring out His judgment on Israel, He wasn't going to do it tranquilly where nobody would notice. Amos brazenly astonished the Hebrews in calling two pagan nations to witness the debasement of Israel. There are two idyllic reasons for this rhetorical device. First, these nations are the epitome of evil in Hebrew perspective, yet they will judge Israel's misdeeds. Using these ancient enemies felt like rubbing salt on open wound. God is insinuating the pagans were currently morally superior to His chosen children. Secondly, they behaved beyond the standards of even international decency, so correction by enemies embarrassed them.

The mountain view of Samaria provided a magnificent vantage point for observing what transpired in the city. It should be noted these nations were to the south and would have been Assyria's next conquest. These evil nations observed injustice had become second nature to people in Israel. The people didn't even know how to do what was right. His weapon of judgment is total humiliation. Everything Israel held dear was destroyed. Everything they had confidence in was taken away. They were left with nothing—destroyed, captured, and humiliated.

Once again, God is picturing Himself as a lion. Except this time, He has just devoured His prey. He left a couple of legs and a piece of the lamb's ear. Here is the promised remnant.

When God's weapon of judgment is used on the local churches today, they also become a reproach to the own communities.

> Therefore, thus says the LORD God: "An adversary shall be all around the land; He shall sap your strength from you, and your palaces shall be plundered." Thus says the Lord: "As a shepherd takes from the mouth of a lion two legs or a piece of an ear, so shall the children of Israel be

> taken out Who dwell in Samaria—In the corner of a bed and on the edge of a couch! Hear and testify against the house of Jacob," says the LORD God, the God of hosts. (Amos 3:11–13 NKJV)

As usual, starting the sentence with *therefore* draws a conclusion from previous information. The prior section tells us the palaces and strongholds of Israel stored up violence and plunder. Now these strongholds will be destroyed to the point only a small remnant will remain. Such is the meaning of the shepherd's allegory about portions of sheep left to prove predation. Amos has emphasized corporate judgment of nations. This pattern holds true whether we're talking about ancient Israel, modern nations, or the local church today. God corporately judges those entities that rebel against Him. Especially when He has poured out His blessing on them. This is how He deals with groups of people. These verses give a glimpse of God dealing with the individuals within the corporate structure. In the verses we just read, God gave a very graphic picture of what happens. Once again God is picturing Himself as a lion. Except this time, He has just devoured His prey. He left a couple of legs and a piece of the lamb's ear. Here is the promised remnant. Even though the nation was destroyed and brought to its knees in humility, some individuals within the nation would be spared.

> "That in the day I punish Israel for their transgressions, I will also visit destruction on the altars of Bethel; And the horns of the altar shall be cut off and fall to the ground. I will destroy the winter house along with the summer house; The houses of ivory shall perish, And the great houses shall have an end," says the Lord. (Amos 3:14–15 NKJV)

The reference to the royal sanctuary altar at Bethel was no surprise. Bethel was the beginning of idolatrous worship in the Northern

Kingdom. Places defiled by heresy and substitute faith were torn down consistently in the Old Testament. The stunning revelation is cutting the horns of the altar. These horns were artificial projections on the outside corners resembling the horns of an ox. Their purpose related to the right of sanctuary in fleeing from an enemy or oppressor. The sting of these words announces there was no safety for attempts to flee the judgment of God.

Final Thoughts

There is an axiom in the medical profession that states, "All bleeding will stop." How bleeding stops is of greater import to the patient than the practitioners. Remember the conditions in Israel at the time of Amos. The nation as a whole was wealthy, prosperous, and at peace because their enemies were in a worse condition. The affluence of the people will have dampened the impact of the message. I can imagine the people of Samaria simply raising an eyebrow unconcerned about the wounds Amos's prophecies perpetrated. The words must have seemed preposterous when they believed they were blessed. Yet, when judgment is finished, nothing will be left of the nation of Israel.

The altars at Bethel were human institutions created for religious power and became a symbol of the broken relationship between God and Israel. Bethel's altar was a sign of rebellion and an emblem of apostacy. It is ironic that a symbol of faith can become the emblem of a relic dead religion. I fear sometimes the cross of Christ can be used as an icon for prosperity and wealth instead of a place where the believer reckons himself crucified to this world.

Application

1. How do some of the actions of modern Christians offend against God's holiness?

2. What effect does it have on others when Christians corrupt themselves and fail to behave in right ways? (1 Timothy 4:2; Habakkuk. 2:6–11.)

3. What are some of the ways in which people seek comfort in religion? Why is it that special religious clothing and objects cannot save us from God's punishment on sin? (1 Samuel. 15:22; Psalms 51:16–17; Mark 12:33)?

4. Micah 6:8 says Christians are required to walk humbly with their God. How do the pressures of modern life divert us from this?

5. What warnings are there to be seen today of coming judgment from God? (2 Timothy 3:1–9.)

Chapter Five

Spiritual Mad Cow Disease

"There is always more misery among the lower classes than there is humanity in the higher."[9]
—*Victor Hugo*

"The quest for riches darkens the sense of right and wrong."[10]
—*Antiphanes*

I am seventy-three years old and have been married to Diana for fifty-three years. I know Diana has never considered divorce, but I'm not sure murder ever came off the table. The first time a lady called me misogynist, I reflexively denied the charge, but then went to the dictionary to look the word up. Whatever dog house I wind up in, I do know categorically men and women can speak the same language and have totally different meanings. For example, if your wife asks you. "Do you want to go out for dinner?" The question will have nothing to do with your wants or needs. She is actually saying, "I have had a tough day and don't want to cook or do dishes." When your wife says: "It's your decision." She really means, "I think I've made it perfectly clear what the correct decision is." When she says, "Do whatever you want." She really means, "You'll pay for this later." When she says, "I'll be ready in a minute." She really means, "Relax, it'll be a while." When she says, "You have to learn to communicate." She really means, "agree with me and everything will be fine." And when she says, "Nothing." She really means, "Everything." Even though I may be "feministic challenged," unlike Amos, I would never call a woman a "cow".

---

*In Amos **Chapter Four**, spiritual mad cow disease is an excellent illustration to the sin infecting the wealthy women in Israel.*

Bovine spongiform encephalitis or Mad Cow Disease is caused by protein fragments called a prion which specifically infects nerve tissue. They are difficult to destroy and are not sterilized by methods used for virus and bacteria. The disease has spread throughout the world although the first US case seeped into Washington state in 2003.[11] With no cure, MCD is fatal. MCD is a great allegory for sin infecting the human soul, which will lead to death according to Scripture. In Amos Chapter Four, spiritual mad cow disease is an excellent illustration to the sin infecting the wealthy women in Israel.

> Hear this word, you cows of Bashan, who are on the mountain of Samaria, Who oppress the poor, who crush the needy, who say to your husbands, "Bring wine, let us drink!" (Amos 4:1 NKJV)

At Costco I saw two small frozen Kobe beef steaks for $97. Kobe beef is cherished for its superior flavor, tenderness and high amount of intramuscular fat, giving the meat a marbled appearance. The strange rearing techniques are said to enhance its value. For example: the cows are provided beer to induce appetite, massaged daily often with a sake wine cocktail, and provided classical music for relaxation at feeding time. There is no scientific evidence proving these techniques improve texture and meat flavor, but they certainly make Kobi-pampered cows and expensive meat.

Amos calls the women of Samaria pampered cows similar to Kobe beef. The term "cows of Bashan" designates a breed of cattle famous for the fat in the beef. These animals fed on the fertile plains of what now is known as the Golan Heights above the Sea of Galilee. The insult captured the attention of his audience and allowed the prophet to focus on his message. These women were usurping the husband's leadership while demanding more, like an alcoholic demanding drink. These men provided for their wives' expensive tastes by oppressing poor impoverished fellow Hebrews. In designating location to the "mountains of Samaria," he is limiting the condemnation to the wives of the political and religiously elite. The women are blamed because of their domineering attitude while chewing on a cud of luxury.

Spiritual Mad Cow Disease

> The LORD God has sworn by His holiness: "Behold, the days shall come upon you when He will take you away with fishhooks, and your posterity with fishhooks. You will go out through broken walls, each one straight ahead of her, and you will be cast into Harmon," says the LORD. (Amos 4:2–3 NKJV)

In Amos's culture, swearing by something, augmented some assurance to the oath. Adding God's absolute sovereignty and holiness to the proclamation pushes the weight and importance of the message. God pronounces the ultimate cure for Samaria's mad cow outbreak. He promises every one of these society ladies would be dragged through holes in the city wall instead of the gate. This action equates each mad cow the same social standing as any other city captive. Pictorial reliefs in the British Museum show Assyrian captives led single file with hooks in their faces. The word "cast out" implies the tossing of dead bodies. Amos may be trying to picture an image of the cows of Bashan lying as carrion at the base of Mt. Hermon.

Religious Hypocrisy

> "Come to Bethel and transgress, At Gilgal multiply transgression; Bring your sacrifices every morning, Your tithes every three days. Offer a sacrifice of thanksgiving with leaven, Proclaim and announce the freewill offerings; For this you love, You children of Israel!" Says the Lord God. (Amos 4:4–5 NKJV)

Two problems are delineated here: (1) giving to false gods, and (2) unacceptable offerings. These comments were the result of false worship and social injustice. Amos parodies a priest's call to worship in sarcastic hyperbole. Bethel designated the Northern King's chief sanctuary where a golden calve idol received worship. The prophet chooses the high point in the nation's liturgical life to reveal the low point in their spiritual existence. An invitation to multiply sins of false worship at a pagan shrine. Tithes were set apart to offer every three years, and freewill offerings were occasional. In stressing those as more important than daily offerings and three-day tithes made bragging about these gifts a sham. These religious activities were not in devotion to God but as a show of religious fever to fellow Israelites. Their consistent false worship proved offensive in polluting God's covenant by hypocritical practice while violating the same covenant. The freewill offerings were cheerful celebrations, and Amos stands up and punctures the festive balloon.

Two thirds of all Americans claim to be Christian, but do they go through ceremony without faith or thought? We may read Scripture, recite the Apostle's Creed and the Lord's prayer, and take communion by habit without thought. Have we pretended to listen to sermons and homilies without understanding or application? How many of us are mechanically and superficially practicing faith by rote similar to Amos's Israel? Tibetan prayer wheels are a cylinder with a written prayer of some Lama embossed on the cylinder exterior. The faithful would spin the wheel to send the prayer to heaven thereby earning merit for the life to come. Since the written language is for the priest class, most practitioners have no idea of what is written on each prayer wheel. They spin the wheels respectively with no thought to what is actually prayed; they are simply trying to earn a better placement after death. I wonder how many times you and I have said the Lord's prayer by rote with no thought to the meaning of the words. When we reduce worship to liturgical practice without spiritual relationship, are we not following the path of ancient Northern Israel? Ecclesiastes 5:1 proclaims:

> "Guard your steps when you go into the house of God. To draw near to listen is better than to offer sacrifice of fools, for they do not know that they are doing evil." (ESV)

Five times the Lord says, "Yet you did not return to me."
People should realize we are so corrupted that the Lord needs to slap a two-by-four across our head to get attention once in a while.

Watershed Moments

> "Also I gave you cleanness of teeth in all your cities, and lack of bread in all your places; Yet you have not returned to Me," says the LORD. "I also withheld rain from you, when there were still three months to the harvest. I made it rain on one city, I withheld rain from another city. One part was rained upon, and where it did not rain the part withered. So two or three cities wandered to another city to drink water, but they were not satisfied; Yet you have not returned to Me," Says the LORD "I blasted you with blight and mildew. When

> your gardens increased, your vineyards, your fig trees, and your olive trees, The locust devoured them; Yet you have not returned to Me," says the Lord. "I sent among you a plague after the manner of Egypt; Your young men I killed with a sword, along with your captive horses; I made the stench of your camps come up into your nostrils; Yet you have not returned to Me," says the LORD. "I overthrew some of you, As God overthrew Sodom and Gomorrah, and you were like a firebrand plucked from the burning; Yet you have not returned to Me," says the LORD. (Amos 4:6–11 NKJV)

Five times the Lord says, "Yet you did not return to me". People should realize we are so corrupted that the Lord needs to slap a two-by-four across our head to get attention once in a while. But five times! These disasters were not caused by nature or random chance or even foreign powers. God warned in Leviticus 26 and Deuteronomy 28–29 saying He would use famine, drought, crop failure, plagues, military defeat, and even earthquake devastation as a chastisement anticipating repentance. The five-fold refrain— "yet you did not return to me" (ESV)—underscores Israel's continued obstinacy. Guilt accumulated in their persistent refusal to recognize God's chastisement. "You did not return to me" rings into the epitaph of the nation's history. This Scripture should remind believers that life's experiences and troubles may function as signposts to God's will and pleasure. Of course, not every difficulty or trouble is an explicit divine signpost, yet personal contemplation should help in decisions which honor Christ.

Recently in America we had a toilet paper famine, extreme drought in the southwest, tornados destroying parts of Illinois and Kentucky, snow closures in Hawaii, crop destruction in the farm belt, a humiliating military defeat in Afghanistan, and a Covid 19 pandemic killing over a million Americans. Chignik, Alaska also logged the strongest earthquake of the year at 8.2 on the Richter scale. Things were so tense that people quit shaking hands and started fist or elbow bumping. Some blame the pandemic, but I noticed fist bumping started at the toilet paper shortage. Yet, as to Israel, has God sent warning to a people who have ceased to follow righteous paths? I think maybe God is like a medical doctor probing the patient until he finds the spot that hurts. The doctor needs to get the patient's attention in order to cure a serious problem.

Prepare to Meet Your God

> "Therefore, thus will I do to you, O Israel; Because I will do this to you, prepare to meet your God, O Israel!" For behold, He who forms mountains, and creates the wind, who declares to man what his thought is, and makes the morning darkness, who treads the high places of the earth—The LORD God of hosts is His name. (Amos 4:12-13 NKJV)

The whole point is if you won't meet God in repentance, then you will meet Him in judgment.

"Prepare to meet your God" sounds like a line from an old Clint Eastwood Dirty Harry movie. The phrase is favorite for any would be fire and brimstone preacher but in context to Amos, it has a parallel idea. The whole point is if you won't meet God in repentance, then you will meet Him in judgment. Israel wanted religion without repentance and faith without adherence even after getting message after message. The people persisted in economic exploitation amid religious hypocrisy. If empty stomachs, drought, blight, plagues, military disaster and, earthquakes would not spur return to faith, then final judgment became the only thing left. Often Christians spend ink and voice condemning our fallen world for its obvious sins. Scripturally, God is most concerned about the transgression of those who call upon His name. Simply doing "churchy" things does not prevent the sins of a vapor faith. Many Christians and churches are so busy with religious activities, they often neglect the spiritual and physical needs of those around them. In doing so they are ignoring the clear commands of the God they claim to worship. Maybe a physical/social needs elder should be adopted into each church board and charter.

The last verse of Chapter Four points out the majesty and power of the creator. Yahweh, the Lord of Hosts, is specifically named the one who formed the mountains and blows the winds with thunder—a picture of omnipotent power in the God they were to meet. Apparently, Amos had to define God because the god of Bethel was a golden calf. The knowledge of God experienced such utter pollution, a specification had been needed. In today's multicultural society, we still need to define God in order to communicate evangelism. I think we have sunk further than ancient Israel.

Final Thoughts

We in the western hemisphere have been focused on our own needs and wants. We have gotten so use to wealth, believing we deserve the freedom of accumulation. People are free and entitled to anything labored to possess. The danger is, when intensely focused on our own desires and perceived rights, that we forget all others. The reality is everything we have has been given us, and it originated from our creator. God has been so good, many naively accept an entitlement attitude. Some believe the only helping hand is on their own arm or that God helps those who help themselves. Both opinions are wrong because the Lord gives and the Lord takes away, blessed be the name of the Lord (see Job 1:21).

Seattle, Washington has invented the Seattle Atheist Church by redefining the word church to mean "a community intentionally built around a set of shared values."[12] This is similar to vegans eating animal crackers and wanting their tofu to taste like meat. Mindlessly pretending religious activities is similar to the problem Amos condemns. To Christians, a church building is primarily a place to worship our Lord and Savior Jesus Christ. The universal church is all believers in the saving faith of Jesus Christ, even though we cannot seem to agree on how to worship, but can universally agree on the Apostle's Creed. Scripture says final judgment will come to all of us whether we want to believe it or not. The difference will be those who repent and accept the atoning death of the Lord Jesus Christ will have their punishment borne on the savior Himself. Sadly, those who refuse to be reconciled to God will have no protection to the wrath of God. Hebrews 10:31 say "It is a fearful thing to fall into the hands of the living God" (NKJV) Every human being must decide how to meet God—on His terms or our own. How you intend to meet Him is most important question in life.

Applications

1. Read Deuteronomy 28. Read Leviticus 26:13–18. What are the disasters the Lord promised to bring upon his people if they failed him?

2. Can you think of any attitudes of entitlement within today's Christian church.

3. What should our attitude be when severe trouble comes upon us?

4. How can we use the events happening around us to call people to repentance?

5. How can a message of judgment be merciful?

Chapter Six

The Walking Dead

"A single death is a tragedy; a million deaths is a statistic."
—Joseph Stalin[13]

"I know your works.
You have the reputation of being alive, but you are dead."
—Revelations 3:1 ESV

This chapter is not about the Zombie Apocalypse. Amos preaches Israel's funeral while they are still living. One of the most famous premature obituaries prompted the Mark Twain comment, "Reports of my death have been greatly exaggerated." Apple's Steve Jobs was accorded the longest premature obituary in a seventeen-page Bloomberg[14] piece accidentally distributed three years before his death. At least Wall Street reacted to Steve Jobs's obituary, whereas Israel ignored their obit when Amos announced it. Amos Chapter Five is a eulogy for the living, walking dead even though the actual events are still thirty years into their future. The passage is a lament or poem of mourning. Jeremiah's book of Lamentations is a poem about the death and destruction of Jerusalem.

While ministering in a Cowboy Church, I learned a new term called a "Texas Longhorn Sermon." A Longhorn sermon is where there is a point up front, another point way at the end, and a whole lot of bull in between. Amos's style is the exact opposite of the Longhorn sermon with the important point right in the center. Chapter five of Amos starts with a chiasm, a type of poetic structure that repeats ideas in parallel with the main thought in the center. Note that verses 1–3 are similar to verses 16–17 and verses 5–6 parallel verses 14–15. This structure makes verses 7–13 the meat or main idea of this verbal sandwich. The beauty of a chiasm is to put focus of the poem into the middle section. Think of it like an Oreo cookie; the stuff on the outside supports the important stuff in the middle. As we walk through the chiasm, let's bundle the information into three points. First point for the walking dead is that destruction is imminent. Second is that hope is available. Third is evil is abounding, but God is still sovereign.

Death Through Inertia

> Hear this word, Israel, this lament I take up concerning you: "Fallen is Virgin Israel, never to rise again, deserted in her own land, with no one to lift her up." This is what the Sovereign Lord says to Israel: "Your city that marches out a thousand strong will have only a hundred left; your town that marches out a hundred strong will have only ten left."
>
> Therefore, this is what the Lord, the Lord God Almighty, says: "There will be wailing in all the streets and cries of anguish in every public square. The farmers will be summoned to weep and the mourners to wail. There will be wailing in all the vineyards, for I will pass through your midst," says the Lord. (Amos 5:1–3, 16–17 NIV)

The objective of this chapter is to impress upon God's people the impossibility of averting destruction and focus those self-secure sinners on the false sandy foundation of their porous faith. In order to emphasize the dirge, Amos utters it in the tonal meter of the traditional funeral service. Previously we have seen that certain judgment shadows the Northern Kingdom of Israel with a call to repentance. In Chapter Five things bode even more serious. Death is a done deal. Judgment is now imminent, and the dirge treats her like she is dead and in the grave. Verse one states that when Israel falls, not even God will come to her rescue. God will destroy a nation for corporate sins but is still concerned about the individual people. The nation is spoken as dead. But who will survive in the ten percent remnant? Unrepentant, a thousand will march proudly out, crawling back with a ninety percent loss even though she was warned in unmistakable terms. It was no idle threat, the Sovereign Lord Himself declared the result.

The theme of destruction returns in verses 16 and 17 so vast that the entire population mourns and wails. Village streets and farms are involved in the misery. Notice that even professional mourners cannot be hired, so the farmers are called from the fields to mourn the dead. The mourning of the dead is so universal that there is not enough personnel to fulfill the normal funeral rites.

Verse seventeen uses two very unique verbal images. Harvest time was a time of song, feasting, and rejoicing especially in the vineyards (see Isaiah 16:10). God "passing through" their midsts references the Passover in Egypt where God passed through the Egyptians, killing the first born. This emphasized that there is no special redemption for the Hebrews of Israel.

Hope is Available with Justice

> This is what the LORD says to Israel: "Seek me and live; do not seek Bethel, do not go to Gilgal, do not journey to Beersheba. For Gilgal will surely go into exile, and Bethel will be reduced to nothing." Seek the LORD and live, or he will sweep through the tribes of Joseph like a fire; it will devour them, and Bethel will have no one to quench it.

> Seek good, not evil, that you may live. Then the LORD God Almighty will be with you, just as you say he is. Hate evil, love good; maintain justice in the courts. Perhaps the LORD God Almighty will have mercy on the remnant of Joseph. (Amos 5:4–6, 14–15 NIV)

The theme of Chapter Five is the difference between true religion and false faith in God. I escaped graduate school as an atheist with three framed wall parchment sheets and found employment as a research biologist. A few years later I had a beautiful wife and two kids and couldn't reconcile the existences of love or good and evil with my atheistic world view. I found the only logical explanation for the universe was a Creator God. That revelation started my search that eventually led to Jesus Christ and then seminary to learn His word. Before Richard Dawkins or Christopher Hitchens spewed their atheism, the major spokesman for the non-believing community was Anthony Flew. Flew was the world's most famous atheist at end of the twentieth century. But in 2004, Antony Flew[15] shocked his world by suddenly proclaiming a belief in God. Flew, like most atheists, had been a chronological snob in saying that man no longer needs to believe in God or gods because the age of science and reason had brought enlightenment. Flew lost his atheistic faith because he was influenced by the statistical and ontological argument of Einstein. He came to believe the universe must have had an intelligent designer. Unfortunately, Antony Flew never sought further than believing in a higher power before his death in 2011. He did not search for God, but was content to stay in spiritual ignorance.

If God is not on the throne, then man places himself there.
Do orchestras really need conductors?

Verse 4 says "seek and live". Does not *seeking* mean search for something lost or inaccessible? When Yahweh God is the subject, it means to turn to Him as a way of life as a sovereign. If God is not on the throne, then man places himself there. Do orchestras really need conductors? With no conductor, we can play any tune we want, any way we want, any place we want. The "seek" request was to find the conductor instead of the auditorium. Amos claims the people's faith was in ritual worship and shrines instead of the God of Scripture.

Bethel was the location where Jacob first wrestled with God and the shrine became the prime location of the golden calf worship in the Northern Kingdom of Israel. *Bethel* actually means *House of God* and Amos says it will be reduced to *Beth Aven* or *house of nothing* in the Hebrew. Gilgal was the location of Joshua's monument for crossing the Jordan and entering the promised land. Amos says Gilgal will go from *entrance* to *exile*. Both statements would be a cultural shock to his audience. A repentant heart changes direction away from sin, not simply sorry about sin. Theologically we need to remember that men are forgiven *when* they repent, not *because* they repent.

The root of the social problems is not flawed social organization, but sin. Society cannot make fundamental improvements by changing the environment, but only by a change in the hearts of men. Much of the present-day preoccupation of churches with such things as better housing, improved standards of living, etc., has resulted from the failure to behold this truth. No matter what social planners and environmentalists may say, there is no escaping the fact that all of man's problems originated in Eden, and there was nothing at all wrong with that environment. The entry of sin was the destructive factor that drowned the whole world in woe.

Pastor Roy Ratcliff is the Church of Christ minister who was called upon one day to come and baptize an inmate at a federal prison in Wisconsin. That inmate was Jeffrey Dahmer, the infamous killer who had been sentenced to fifteen consecutive life terms for a series of heinous murders in the Milwaukee area. Convicted of killing seventeen men and boys between 1978 and 1990, Dahmer's slayings were notorious for being particularly gruesome. Some of the murders involved acts of dismemberment, necrophilia, and even cannibalism. After going on trial in July 1992 and being found guilty and sane on fifteen counts of murder, the convicted killer was sentenced to fifteen life terms, a total of 943 years in prison. This killer served his sentence at Columbia Correctional Institute in Portage, Wisconsin, where he became increasingly religious and eventually announced that he had become a born-again Christian. For seven months after Dahmer's behind-bars baptism, Pastor Ratcliff visited him weekly for discipleship and Bible study to nurture his growth as a Christian. And, although the convicted felon died in November 1994, beaten to death by a fellow inmate, the minister who spent time with Dahmer proclaimed he died a changed believer.[16] If Jeffery Dahmer can be changed, our social problems are corrected by one life at a time finding truth in Jesus Christ.

Evil Social Injustice Exists

> There are those who turn justice into bitterness and cast righteousness to the ground. He who made the Pleiades and Orion, who turns midnight into dawn and darkens day into night, who calls for the waters of the sea and pours them out over the face of the land—the LORD is his name. With a blinding flash he destroys the stronghold and brings the fortified city to ruin. There are those who hate the one who upholds justice in court and detest the one who tells the truth. You levy a straw tax on the poor and impose a tax on their grain. Therefore, though you have built stone mansions, you will not live in them; though you have planted lush vineyards, you will not drink their wine. For I know how many are your offenses and how great your sins. There are those who oppress the innocent and take bribes and deprive the poor of justice

in the courts. Therefore, the prudent keep quiet in such times, for the times are evil. (Amos 5:7–13 NIV)

Remember the chiastic design of the Hebrew eulogy. Here in the center is where the virtue and accomplishments of the dead would be extolled. Our redneck prophet turns the eulogy alarming. The Amos's contemporary, Isaiah, said:

Woe to those who call evil good and good evil, who put darkness for light and light for darkness, who put bitter for sweet and sweet for bitter. (Isaiah 5:20 NIV)

When Christians think moral issues are relevant to everyday life, we focus on things like abortion, homosexuality, family identity issues. How many of us think about economic issues as moral? Evangelicals are split into two distinct camps. One group focuses on an evangelistic gospel wanting souls saved around the world. The other focuses on the church transforming society. In reality both camps are New Testament concepts, but society can only change one person at a time; changing one heart at a time is the only successful way of changing one culture at a time. Clearly we need to go both directions. You can't have a culture that isn't made of individuals, and individuals bring their own dimension to the culture. So that means that the problem is a personal problem. It's not ultimately a societal problem. You cannot change society by external means, top down. The only way to transform society is bottom up, meaning a culture change is by changed lives. That means renewed hearts via Jesus Christ. This passage should be a warning to any nation, church or individual.

The only way to transform society is bottom up, meaning a culture change is by changed lives. That means renewed hearts via Jesus Christ.

The term *bitterness* is literally *wormwood* as translated in the KJV. Wormwood is bitter and associated with poison. The judicial system instead of being medicinal to heal wrongs and restore rights has poisoned the nation. Righteousness is shoved prostrate on the ground with no one to raise it up and support it. Verse 7 describes the transmission of poison as unrighteous disease.

The next verses contrast what the Creator God can do instead of poisoning the justice system. The constellation Pleaides dominated the spring and summer months and Orion the fall and winter. The Lord carries all the power in the universe. No power or fortified city can withstand His power because He controls the elements.

The Apostle John said:

> This is the verdict: Light has come into the world, but men loved darkness instead of light because their deeds were evil." (John 3:19 NIV)

Light exposes what things are really like. There are some people who fight hard to keep things in the dark. Israel had the zeal to illegally profit off the poor and hated any righteous judge or witness who told the truth. Verse 13 says the venom of disagreement was so strong that many felt it prudent to just stay silent. The problem of silence is that abusers are freed from opposition and compound their transgressions. Edmund Burke's famous saying, "All it needs for evil to prevail is for good men to do nothing."[17] A silent church has proliferated great confusion in our current times.

Even in the church, we have twisted, pulled, inverted, and denied Scripture in order to make people feel less guilty and more inclusive. In our own churches we have people who preach, sing, and play music yet still live vile and immoral lives. But according to Amos, judgment is coming for those who switch darkness for light. The wrath of God is not from some capricious outburst, but announced, proclaimed, and abstained until the end.

It needs to be pointed out that a direct correlation exists between a godless individual and wickedness. Right and wrong must be filtered through a transformed and purified mind and heart. This happens only with relationship with our creator, Jesus Christ.

We live in a world that can invent bombs to exterminate millions in a moment, yet cannot defeat a single virus. A world where men pontificate on atheism yet they don't even know how their cell phone works.

Ultimate Result

Therefore, this is what the Lord, the LORD God Almighty says: "There will be wailing, in all the streets and cries of anguish in every public square. The farmers will be summoned to weep and the mourners to wail. There will be wailing in all the vineyards, for I will pass through your midst," says the LORD. (Amos 5:16–17 NIV)

God says when judgment comes, it will be everywhere and full. There will not be enough paid mourners to handle the dead. Even farmers will be called out to mourn the dead. The harvest time will not be a time of rejoicing or celebration because God will not *pass over* Israel but *pass through* Israel. It should awaken every believer to realize God does not change or evolve like society wants Him too. The situation of ancient Israel is same news heading as today.

Final Thoughts

Our current culture is desperately ill and in moral crisis. In recent years the wealthy have become richer and the poor poorer. Human sexuality is so confused with Facebook's fifty-six different gender options that our young don't know which bathroom to use. A recent Supreme Court nominee was unable to define what is a woman. And it all comes from a problem where people no longer fear, honor, or respect God or Scripture. We live in a world that can invent bombs to exterminate millions in a moment, yet cannot defeat a single virus, a world where men pontificate on atheism, yet they don't even know how their cell phone works. It is time for good men to stand against evil.

Application

1. What guidance would you give to someone who is seeking to please God solely through ceremonial religion?

2. Can a person be born again if he or she does not give any evidence of a life changed for the better?

3. Search your own heart in church service. Do you just enjoy the rhythm and melody of the songs you sing in church, or do you really enter into the heart of worship? Does the beat of the band's percussion make a bigger impact upon you than the words that you sing?

4. How can we avoid incorporating false gods into Christian worship? How can success, affluence and materialism contaminate our worship of God?

Chapter Seven

Let Justice Roll Down Like Water

*"Before you attempt to beat the odds,
be sure you could survive the odds beating you."*[18]
—Larry Kersten

I once, inadvertently, told a gathering of Chinese government officials and business men that they were going to hell. In China it is generally illegal and culturally inappropriate for a western minister to preach to the Chinese public. But one of the local churches organized a gathering of people interested in the American Christmas and Christian beliefs. As an American school principal and ordained minister, I commanded social respect and influence in our community. I was asked to be the major speaker. These people were the intellectuals and leaders of the community. I perceived an excellent opportunity to share the gospel. I chose an idea borrowed from C. S. Lewis's *Mere Christianity*[19] explaining why Christians believe Jesus as God in the flesh. No one can call Jesus a "good man," because Jesus himself claimed to be God our Creator. Anyone who claims to be God is either a lunatic equal to the guy who believes he a potted plant or a lying con-man or exactly whom he claimed to be—God himself. We cannot call Jesus a "good man," because anybody who claims to be God takes the "good man" idea off the table. I considered this concept to be an acceptable approach to a thinking public audience, and I worked diligently on my cross-cultural message. I had learned only survival Mandarin and chose to use a translator from the local church in order to properly convey the message. Precept by precept I clarified, pausing between every sentence or two waiting for my translator to elucidate correctly. Formulating a call to action at the end, I said something like: "Christians believe Jesus Christ is exactly whom He claimed to be, God in flesh. But as thinking men, you must choose yourself which of the three options you think this Jesus could be: A con artist, a lunatic, or God, as He claimed." As usual, my translator relayed my last comment. Yet then he kept speaking for another minute of two. I turned to him confused, and he said, "Oh, I hope you don't mind, but I told them if they don't accept Christ, they are going to burn in hell forever."

Even though not my intended presentation, I recognized God is sovereign, and possibly a strong ending could be culturally necessary. Amos also must have had God's leading to approach Israel with strong words.

Sixty-seven percent of Stanford University MBA students believed they were above the median of their classmates, and eighty-seven percent of Frenchmen say they are above average lovers. Belief is not necessarily reality.

We can't look at the next portion of Amos without bringing up the concept of assumed overconfidence. For example, surveys show sixty-five percent of all Americans believe they are above average intelligence. Sixty-seven percent of Stanford University MBA students believed they were above the median of their classmates and eighty-seven percent of Frenchmen say they are above average lovers.[20] Belief is not necessarily reality. And the nation of Israel believed their ancestral relationship with God kept them from judgment. They expected to profit on the day, but Amos confronts their hypocritical religion ideas.

A kindergarten teacher was receiving Christmas gifts from her pupils. The florist's son handed her a long box. She shook it overhead and said, "I bet you gave me roses."

"That's right!" said the boy. "But, how did you know?"

"Oh, just a wild guess," she said.

The candy shop's daughter next held out her gift. "Oh, I bet that's box of chocolates."

She beamed. "That's right, but how did you know?" asked the girl.

"Oh, just a wild guess," said the teacher.

The next gift was from the son of the liquor storeowner. The teacher held the package overhead, but it was leaking. She caught a drop of leakage with her finger and put it to her tongue. "Is it wine?" she asked.

"No," the boy replied, with some excitement. "It's a puppy!"

Assumptions can have consequences we may not appreciate.

An erroneous assumption, common to humanity, is believing good deeds provide merit before a loving god. Scripturally, the things accumulated while here on earth, mean nothing at the gates of heaven. We in ourselves have no standing or merit with any credible position before God. When we can recognize God's existence at all times and in all things, then true fear of God rules the heart. So instead of looking at our accomplishments and congratulating them, we say, "This is the work of the Lord."

It's difficult to deny the fact we live in a country drifting away from a previous haven for moral and ethical lifestyles, but now surging through a tsunami of immorality. We have seen human depravity exposed in living color, broadcast live on screen with every newscast. Amos, too, couldn't believe his eyes either, living in the midst of great injustice with complete disobedience to God's commandments. The people of Israel still held their ceremonies and worship rituals without any linkage to the God of Scripture. As we ourselves have witnessed, when God is expelled from culture, no moral anchor is left. God spoke through our redneck prophet saying, "I can't stand what I see. Change your ways or quit bogus worship"

The Day of the Lord

> Alas, you who are longing for the day of the Lord, for what purpose will the day of the Lord be to you? It will be darkness and not light: As when a man flees from a lion And a bear meets him, or goes home, leans his hand against the wall and a snake bites him. Will not the day of the Lord be darkness instead of light, even gloom with no brightness in it? (Amos 5:18–20 NASB)

The term "day of the Lord" is repeated twenty-five times in eleven different books throughout the Bible, including the books of Isaiah, Ezekiel, Joel, Amos, Obadiah, Zephaniah, Zechariah, Malachi, Acts, 1 & 2 Thessalonians, and 2 Peter. A common complaint in biblical literature is that bad people can prosper while God allows the innocent to suffer. During my atheist years, one of my major complaints was asking why a righteous, good God allows evil to exist. One day I took an honest look at myself in a mirror and was glad God had patience in judgment, knowing I had an evil heart, but relieved I found a Savior in Jesus Christ. But God will not always remain patient and remote. He will deal with the unrighteousness of all men when He reconciles accounts on the day of the Lord.

The truth Amos proclaims is Israel had also become God's enemy.

Israels fervor for the day of the Lord is emphasized in the phrase translated *long for*, which elsewhere is translated *hunger* and *thirst* and even *greed* in the Proverbs. Amos corrects their understanding that it will be a dark time instead of bright for all unjustified. The illustrations are concepts of disaster and safety instead of clarifying righteous and wicked. To the Northern kingdom, they believed it announced a time

Let Justice Roll Down Like Water

of vengeance upon enemies when the Lord will fight on their behalf. In eagerly anticipating the day, the people did not realize judgment would fall on them as well as the wicked nations surrounding them. The truth Amos proclaims is Israel had also become God's enemy. The old verbiage, "out of the frying pan into the fire" is an apt concept for verse 19. These verses remind me of the coyote and road runner cartoons where any planned escape falls into something worse. Runnings from a lion into an angry bear then finding a place of rest get bitten by a snake.

I remember an event from the days of the Exxon Valdez clean up in Prince William Sound. A calculation found an $80,000 price tag each to rehabilitate oil covered sea otters.[21] Two were released with fanfare and television coverage only to be eaten by a pod of killer whales in full view of environmental America.

The allegory demonstrates no safety from judgment will be found at the day of the Lord. Amos's last question emphatically illustrates this concept. There is no refuge from God except the refuge found in Christ. For many, the day of the Lord will be going from bad to worse.

No Justice—No Worship

> "I hate, I reject your festivals, nor do I delight in your solemn assemblies. Even though you offer up to Me burnt offerings and your grain offerings, I will not accept them; And I will not even look at the peace offerings of your fatlings. Take away from Me the noise of your songs; I will not even listen to the sound of your harps." (Amos 5:21–23 NASB)

Amos laments that God nor even the Bible is remembered in their services. People following God of Scripture found their lifestyle abhorrent. I've read social justice commentators trying to claim these verses relate to not taking care of the poor and indigent. Amos has already pointed out that social decay is a symptom of forgetting our Creator.

A heart changed by Christ cannot judge people by color, geography, or economic status. God rejects their worship because of impure hearts not deeds.

Today Christian services are calculated to please the congregants more than to please God. At the end of the service people will say, "It was a good service." Was it really good in God's sight? Worship in the western church has become the elephant in the room. The great cathedrals are empty on Sunday, and local pastors preach to vacant pews. Folks actually searching for fellowship become polarized in their ideas of worship. Is the service traditional or non-traditional? Are services structured or non-structured? Do you sing hymns, choruses, or both? Do we confuse music and singing for worship? Do you do things in a very structured way, or are you a more unstructured group? As fallen humans we can polarize something that is not polarized in scripture. Worship should be enjoyably dignified, but not dull. My old preaching instructor, Haddon Robinson, once told our seminary class that he believed God thought it a great sin to move a congregation to boredom with the Bible. Biblical worship moves body, mind, and soul to reverence Jesus Christ.

A paramedic on a Texas talk show told of his most interesting experience. He said a church deacon called 911 saying a man died during the worship service. The paramedic entered the sanctuary stealthy in order to not interrupt the sermon. He said their team disturbed four sleeping gentlemen before they actually found the dead man. Polarized groups will call dignity dull or enthusiasm as irreverent. Real worship has to discover something between a circus and a funeral with Jesus as the focus.

The Westminster Catechism proclaims the chief end of man is to "glorify God, and to enjoy Him forever." Like Amos proclaimed to the Israelites, we must worship the correct God and worship Him correctly. Song and services that praise yourself, loves yourself, and glorifies yourself fall frighteningly short of glorifying God. Jesus told the Samaritan woman, "Yet a time is coming and has now come when the true worshipers will worship the Father in spirit and truth" (see John 4:23 NIV).

People who realize their existence is for worshiping God will not prize the things of this earth.

Here is the key to worship, spirit, and truth—not necessarily where we worship or time of worship, not necessarily some holy building, holy site, holy rooms, or holy days. Every morning above the grave is a day of worship. We worship Him the way we dress. We worship Him when we send our children to school or on the way to the office. We worship Him in the way we greet our employees and co-workers. We worship Him mowing the lawn and taking out the garbage. Worship Him in every aspect of our lives. When this is not understood, God is assigned to a box to be pulled out only on Sundays. We start a slide into the trap Amos exposes. To some, attending church has become a meaningless ceremony, attending by habit. Instead, worship must be spiritual, involving the heart; but also, according to Jesus, it must be scriptural involving rational thinking. Otherwise, we can fall under Amos's *woe* where our church services and offerings are a bunch of noise with prayer bouncing off the roof. The elephant in the room becomes a white elephant.

People who realize their existence is for worshiping God will not prize the things of this earth. This is a Christian super power and a difficult concept for unbelievers to grasp. I watched Mother Teresa visit Phoenix, Arizona, in 1982. She walked the poor areas wrapped an old cardigan sweater with two pockets. A television cameraman, emotionally taken by her ministry, put two one-hundred-dollar bills into her hand. She did not even look at the gift but assigned it all wadded up into her pocket. She later found a homeless man living on the streets. The sainted lady simply reached into her pocket and gave the money to the homeless man. The money, to her, serves simply as a tool for others. The chagrined photographer was shocked, because she did not put the same value on earthly matters as he did.

Our redneck prophet already outlined the deeds anathema to the Lord earlier in the book of Amos. They include enslaving people to pay off tiny debts, disregarding the needy, and engaging in unscrupulous commercial activities. The powerful preyed on the weak and changed society's practices so that the wealthy grew wealthier at the expense of the poor. Israel's people would offer their sacrifices in the face of injustice and inequity. They didn't question the system, and they didn't care about the poor. God, on the other hand, was concerned about the impoverished. Amos brought their predicament to the attention of God's people and pushed them to care for the destitute.

Offerings were a part of worship. That is one of the ways that they were to worship. The sacrifices became something that they might simply undergo as ritual. They had commenced worshipping different gods and sacrificing to them also. Gifts and sacrifices were nothing to them anymore. Our society is influenced by the corrupt notions of God. The names have changed, but the false gods they have represented have not changed. Instead of Baal, instead of Ashera, we worship supermodels and their sexuality. Instead of silver, gold, and wood idols, we have many other philosophies drawn from the same sewer of Canaanite deities and the gods of culture.

> "But let justice roll down like waters and righteousness like an ever-flowing stream." (Amos 5:24 NASB)

Every time I read verse 24 I think of Martin Luther King Jr.'s famous message proclaiming, "let justice flow like water, and righteousness, like an unfailing stream." Dr. King spoke these words one warm summer day in 1963.[22] A phrase from Amos 5 became the rallying cry for a movement of justice for people of color all across this country. Today we can both rejoice in the fact that to a significant degree, Dr. King's wonderful dream has come true. On the one hand, only racists want to divide people by melanin skin content or eye shape. On the other hand, there remain parts of that dream that are still only that—a dream. There are racists on both sides of the political spectrum using skin pigment for political and commercial gain. These are the ones who fall under God's condemnation in the book of Amos.

And He wanted people to be freed from the uncleanness of sin. Only then would the expected deeds of love and justice flow like "an unstoppable stream."

God wanted his people's joy to culminate in blessing. He did not want their acts of justice and righteousness to ooze out of them, but rather he wanted them to flow like brooks that flow down the mountain. And He wanted people to be freed from the uncleanness of sin. Only then would the expected deeds of love and justice flow like "an unstoppable stream." God wanted a day-to-day life of surging integrity and goodness. Only this outer evidence of inner righteousness could offer the Israelites the possibility of survival in the day of the Lord.

Change Your Conduct

> "Did you present Me with sacrifices and grain offerings in the wilderness for forty years, O house of Israel. You also carried along Sikkuth your king and Kiyyun, your images, the star of your gods which you made for yourselves. Therefore, I will make you go into exile beyond Damascus," says the LORD, whose name is the God of hosts. (Amos 5:25–27 NASB)

Notice that the Lord is not saying that these offerings in themselves are wrong; it is the condition of the people's hearts and their disregard for the welfare of the people that is sinful. Isaiah says 'I have more than enough of burnt offerings . . . I have no pleasure in the blood of bulls and lambs and goats' (Isaiah. 1:11 NIV).

Amos is contrasting the true initial faith in the wilderness with the false worship examined earlier. These gods (Sikkuth and Kiyyun) refer to Saturn, the major light in the sky after the sun and the moon. So now they not only failed to worship the Lord with a pure heart, but also embraced false gods in their worship.

Final Thoughts

John Bunyan closes *Pilgrim's Progress*, he does so with a staggering statement: "Then I saw that there was a way to hell, even from the gate of heaven, as well as from the City of Destruction."[23]

You cannot put in separate drawers your relationship with Christ and your relationship with your neighbors. Worship is only meaningful when accompanied by moral ethics and social justice. Faith is more than a building and liturgical services. God's indictment of Israel's social injustice could not be stronger than the message of Amos 5. Ceremonial religion can never safeguard the truth nor guarantee the people to the truth. The evidence of true religion is that it touches all facet of life with holiness, justice, and mercy by obedience to the Word of God.

Applications

1. List liturgical practices that may become simply ritual without holy essence.

2. Analyze your church and its relationship to social justice in your community.

3. What qualities make a person righteous?

Chapter Eight

Smug Snug Humbugs

"Hypocrite: the man who murdered both his parents, pleaded for mercy on the grounds that he was an orphan."[24]
—Abraham Lincoln

Woe to you who are at ease in Zion, and trust in Mount Samaria, . . . go over to Calneh and see; And from there go to Hamath the great; Then go down to Gath of the Philistines. Are you better than these kingdoms? Or is their territory greater than your territory? Woe to you who put far off the day of doom, who cause the seat of violence to come near; Who lie on beds of ivory, stretch out on your couches, Eat lambs from the flock And calves from the midst of the stall; Who sing idly to the sound of stringed instruments, and invent for yourselves musical instruments like David; Who drink wine from bowls, and anoint yourselves with the best ointments, but are not grieved for the affliction of Joseph. Therefore, they shall now go captive as the first of the captives, and those who recline at Banquets shall be removed. (Amos 6:1–14 NKJV)

Smug Snug Humbugs

A dictionary noun definition of a *humbug* is split into three ideas: *something intended to delude or deceive; the quality of falseness or deception; a person who is not what he or she claims or pretends to be; impostor.*[25] The notables of both Judah and Israel probably fit all three definitional concepts. In Chapter Four Amos aimed a shot across the "cows of Bashan." In this portion of Scripture, the wealthy men of power get their condemnation and promised judgment. Attention is turned towards complacent leaders and their intoxicated, easy, smug living. The first verse uses the terms *Zion* and *Samaria,* which incriminates both Amos's Southern Kingdom and Israel's Northern Kingdom. All are getting hit by two *woes*. The noble men represent the elites of the world who have put their sense of security in worldly things. These give them a false sense of security, believing heaven has safety deposit boxes, and their hearse pulls a U-Haul.

We have already learned they had courts without justice and judges without judgment, now elites without empathy.

Both Zion and Mt. Samaria were hill tops claiming military high ground and thought to be militarily impregnable. The security of both nations rested in financial influence, military power, and position, instead of a deep-seated trust in their Creator. Verse two mentions three gentile cities just as prosperous, just as defendable, and with no special status with God. The argument being their trust in circumstance is no better than the pagans around them. Under Jeroboam II, Calneh and Hamath probably fell to Northern Israel in 2 Kings 14. Gath fell to Uzziah in 2 Chronicles 26:6. Through recent events, God demonstrates there is no lasting security in wealth, position, or military might.

With their false premise of safety, life was luxurious and immoral. Never did these citizens believe their lifestyle could affect their nation's safety. The eat, drink, and be merry indulgent banquet image painted is contrasted to the "affliction of Joseph." Remember Joseph was sold into slavery by his own brothers, later to be falsely imprisoned. One of the saddest scenes in Joseph's story is that Ruben who wanted to rescue Joseph, actually did nothing. So is this image of Israel so content among themselves, even those citizens who could care, did nothing. The rich and wealthy smugly enjoyed a luxurious standard of living, while others existed in absolute poverty. Immediate goals were physical pleasures with no thought other than self-indulgence. These were the men of importance and power. Their forgotten charge was to protect their brothers and sisters from exploitation. We have already learned they had courts without justice and judges without judgment, now elites without empathy.

Verse seven gives the statement of God's judgment: if the notable men want to be first in everything, they can be first in judgment.

Unplugged Humbugs

Verses eight through fourteen read like a compendium of Amos's messages in short bites. Exile is still the ultimate destination of the prophecy, but there are intermediate aspects towards this future conquest. These verses are like a rhyming, echo, or retelling of past messages.

> The Lord GOD has sworn by Himself, The LORD God of hosts says: "I abhor the pride of Jacob, and hate his palaces; Therefore, I will deliver up the city and all that is in it." (Amos 6:8 NKJV)

Pride of Jacob

Mohammed Ali was on a plane, and as he didn't have his seat belt fastened, the attendant came up to him and told him to buckle up. "Superman don't need no seat belt," he told her.

She gave him a withering look and said, "Superman don't need no airplane."

The *American Collegiate Dictionary* defines *pride* as a *high or inordinate opinion of one's own dignity, importance, merit, or superiority*. We use terms like egotistical, arrogant, selfish, vain, conceited, boastful, and fat head. When Christians think about pride, generally two things come to mind. First is Proverbs 16:18 (NKJV), "Prides goes before destruction, and a haughty spirit before stumbling." The second is one of the seven deadly sins.

In reality, biblical theologians can designate between two different aspects of pride—good pride and evil pride. The good kind of pride is like what Paul had for some of the New Testament churches; the evil kind is what got Satan cast out of heaven. Maybe it is good to have pride in the accomplishment of others, but not in ourselves. Paul wrote:

Christians are not supposed to think less of themselves,
they just think of themselves less.

"Let nothing be done through selfish ambition or conceit. But in lowliness of mind let each esteem others better than himself. Let each of you should look out not only for his own interests, but also for the interests of others." (Philippians 2:3–4 NKJV)

There is good pride, but the problem is when it is out of balance with humility.

We need to balance pride with humility. You can be proud of your child and have a bumper sticker saying "My child is on the honor list of . . ." But when it comes to showing all the other parents how better your child is than their child, it's a problem. It's all about your motives. If your bumper sticker says, "My child can beat the tar out of your Honor Roll child," your pride probably crosses the line. Amos's comment on the "pride of Jacob" is a pride that proclaims "I can beat the tar out of God in a wrestling match." Christians are not supposed to think less of themselves; they should just think of themselves less.

Jacob's pride included twelve sons, therefore the complete nation is rebuked. The noun translated *places* in verse eight indicates military strongholds. God hates the notion His people would trust in their own strength and power, forgetting a covenant relationship. God's purpose for His people, in every age, is total dependence upon him. And God works in various circumstances so as to achieve that objective in our lives. Our Christian doctrine of sanctification purposes a goal to be like Christ. Live with it, and learn to enjoy His sovereignty.

Plague Post-Apocalypse

> Then it shall come to pass, that if ten men remain in one house, they shall die. And when a relative of the dead, with one who will burn the bodies, picks up the bodies to take them out of the house, he will say to one inside the house, "Are there any more with you?" Then someone will say, "None." And he will say, "Hold your tongue! For we dare not mention the name of the LORD." For behold, the LORD gives a command: He will break the great house into bits, And the little house into pieces. (Amos 6:9–11 NKJV)

Verses nine through eleven proclaim even the survivors don't survive. Our redneck paints a picture of the languishing plague from an extensive siege of Samaria. The dead are exhaustive and overwhelm both the rich and poor, powerful and powerless. Death is the great equalizer for social justice. Current statistics estimate about 69,090,176 people died last year. Which works out to approximately 190857 people a day, 7952 an hour, and 132 people a minute. Which means every second 2 people will die.[26] For every breath you take, approximately seven people have died. Death is everywhere, and it happens to everyone. Mathematicians calculate death; individually it affects one out of every one. I can promise you everyone who reads this book will die. Enough said.

Joseph Stalin said, "a single death is a tragedy, a million deaths are a statistic."[27] In the COVID pandemic, all the world was concentrating only on statistics. Yet I don't know of any family that was not affected by the death of a parent, sibling, aunt, uncle, cousin, or even neighbors. Where is God in the middle of a plague? According to Habakkuk 3, God is before it, in the middle of it, and follows it. That fits the tenth Egyptian plague where He chose to judge as well as giving deliverance.

> "Because thou hast made the LORD, which is my refuge, even the most High, thy habitation; There shall no evil befall thee, neither shall any plague come nigh thy dwelling." (Psalm 91:9–10 KJV)

To the believer, "the LORD gave, and the LORD has taken away; blessed be the name of the Lord" (Job 1:21 NKJV). There is a major difference in the way death affects believers versus non-believers. Death to a believer is simply a change in residence and to the family a hurtful inconvenience. But to the non-believer, death is the end of everything.

In 1527, the bubonic plague hit Martin Luther's home city of Wittenberg, Germany. Luther decided to stay and put his trust in Psalm 91. Luther and his wife Katie opened their home to care for two sick women, and their own son Hans got sick and couldn't eat for three days. Luther's entire household survived the plague, and Katie safely delivered their baby daughter Elizabeth during that siege.

> Do horses run on the rocky crags? Does one plow the sea with oxen? But you have turned justice into poison and the fruit of righteousness into bitterness–you who rejoice in the conquest of Lo-Debar and say, "Did we not take Karnaim by our own strength?" For the Lord God Almighty declares, "I will stir up a nation against you,

that will oppress you all the way from Lebo Hamath to the Valley of the Arabah." (Amos 6:12–14 NIV)

Verse twelve questions assume a *no* answer in a didactic way to demonstrate how perverted justice and righteousness have been turned. The absolute silly situations involved in these questions illustrate the folly of abandoning justice and righteousness for nothing of importance. The two cities taken by military power are a play on words. *Lo Debar* means *thing of nothing* and *Karaim* means *horns*, which symbolize strength. The idea of Amos's word play means by military power you have captured nothing. He has poked a hole in the bloated balloon of military power. In other words, if we go back to the beginning of the passage, the pride of Jacob is worth nothing. Trusting in military advantage is worth nothing.

Final Thoughts

In Ephesians 5:13–14, Paul says

But all things that are exposed are made manifest by the light, for what makes manifest is light. Therefore, He says: "Awake you who sleep, arise from the dead, and Christ will give you light." (NKJV)

The church of Jesus Christ does not recognize male, female, Jew, Gentile or even social standing, much less melanin pigment before the judgment seat of Christ.

Amos is a book that jolts the church from her spiritual slumber and demands a clear response. It is too bad the lunatic fringe has abducted the term *woke* in current society. The above Bible quote would have been a great beginning for the church to shine the light on the injustice in today's world. Some scholars have suggested that Amos is one of the most relevant books of the Old Testament to the modern church. Think about that. God always gives prophetic warning before judgment. Take a lesson from the sinking of the Titanic.

April 15, 1912 (2:20 a.m.) The Titanic sinks. Yet on the eleventh of April, she received six warnings from ships stopped in or passing through heavy ice. Five more warnings came to the Titanic the next day— April 12th. Three more warnings on April thirteenth, and seven more warnings on the fourteenth, the day before the Titanic hit the iceberg! All of these warnings would have been written down as they were intercepted, logged in the radio book, and passed on to the officers on the bridge. There was no way the Captain (Edward John Smith) along with the officers would have been unaware of the huge field of ice that now lay directly in front of them. Incredibly, the Titanic itself actually relayed these warnings back to the shore. Yet the captain of the Titanic thought his ship was unsinkable.

A church fighting racism, poverty, and injustice is a congregation evangelizing individuals for the Kingdom of a soon returning King. The church of Jesus Christ does not recognize male, female, Jew, Gentile, or even social standing, much less melanin pigment before the judgment seat of Christ. Since our Bible defines sin, justice, tolerance, and intolerance, maybe we should take note of all the warnings.

Applications

1. Read the Parable of the Rich Fool in Luke 12:16–21. How did this man show his complacency? What does the Bible say about laziness and its dangers? (See Proverbs 6:9–10, 24:33–34; Isaiah 56:12; Ezekiel 34:2–3.)

2. Notice that it is the things that come out of the mouth which make a person "unclean" (Mark 7:20–23). How is pride related to all the other evil desires in these verses?

3. How can we avoid becoming complacent in our Christian lives?

4. Israel had drifted away from the Lord and His ways. When things go wrong in our personal lives and the life of our churches, what action should be taken?

Chapter Nine

Time to Measure Up

*"Social justice cannot be attained by violence.
Violence kills what it intends to create."*[28]
—Pope John Paul II

A common greeting between Chinese people is literally translated "have you eaten today?" We in the abundant first world have no idea of the social consequences of famine. The Ukraine is the European bread basket accounting for thirty percent of worlds sunflower seed exports, twelve percent of the world's wheat, and seventeen percent of corn. The March 2022 Russian invasion of Ukraine has sent ripples of possible famine in third world countries dependent on Ukraine exports according to Steve Pecsok[29], an assistant professor of economics at Middlebury College. Theses shortages are the result of war. Consider the result of natural disaster such as a locust swarm. A 2020 locust outbreak was putting 5 million Africans at risk of starvation.[30] Deaths would outnumber the Covid-19 pandemic death toll. Contemplate the scare of a locust plague in the agrarian society of Amos's Israel.

---

*Amos knew the locust plague was a righteous judgment
according to the covenant relationship established with Moses.*

Vision One: Locust

> This is what the Lord God showed me: behold, he was forming locusts when the latter growth was just beginning to sprout, and behold, it was the latter growth after the king's mowing's. When they had finished eating the grass of the land, I said, "O Lord God, please forgive! How can Jacob stand? He is so small!" The Lord relented concerning this: "It shall not be," said the Lord. (Amos 7:1–3 ESV)

In this first vision Amos saw that the locusts stripped the land clean of both seeded crops and wild growth. Knowing that the nation would die if this vision became a reality, Amos begged the LORD to forgive the people of their sins. The tragedy of the locust plague is sharpened by its timing. The locusts engulfed the land after the king's share harvest and before the second crop harvest. The king had the right to claim the first cutting of the grain for his military animals (1 Kings 18:5). The "second crop"—either what grew after the first cutting or a separate late planting—was the final growth of the season before the summer's dryness. If it were lost, the people would have nothing to eat until the next harvest.

Amos knew the locust plague was a righteous judgment according to the covenant relationship established with Moses. Yet the vision pulled at his heart. Considering the role of the prophet is to pronounce judgement and mercy, one only needs to look at the ministry of Jesus and the Apostles to see both proclaimed. Even though Amos is being given a message of wrath to proclaim, he still wants repentance in his people. So here he begs God for mercy at the appalling consequence of this vision. Calling Israel "Jacob," Amos intends to remind God of His early commitment to the ancestor when he was at Bethel. (Genesis 28:10–22).

When the Bible says the Lord "relented" or in other versions "repented" we step into a quagmire of theological thought. I want explanations to remain simple and avoid a word salad of philosophical ideas. Therefore, I will put forth the obvious questions, answer them and give an explanation as theologically why? Does God respond to prayer? Yes! Can prayer influence God's actions, wrath or judgements? No!

God's attributes cannot allow Him to be surprised by any unfolding events in time and space. He created mankind for fellowship with Him so intimately that he compares it to marriage in Scripture. His utter holiness requires wrath at sin, engendering to us a Savior to mediate for His rebellious creatures. In giving Amos a vision of the deserved outcome does not invalidate His mercy. He, being God, made the universe, foresaw our rebellion, planned our redemption and has foreknowledge of every prayer request and result that will ever be made. In summary, God is God, and you are not. He responds to prayer because He desires our communion, not some deal making claptrap. In sovereignty, God chooses to use the prayers of His people as the opportunity to bring about the fulfillment of known requests.

God relented because He had already determined that He would relent as a result of Amos's prayer. In every situation God is in perfect control, working out His purposes according to His foreordained plan. Nothing can prevent God from accomplishing that which He has determined to do. God works with us, against us, and even in spite of us. The temptation is to think God's way of accomplishing His ends is to act heedless to our own wants and needs. Not so, He knows our wants and needs before we do. And for those who do not get their wants, remember God's answer to prayer can be no.

God chooses to use the prayers of His people as the opportunity to bring about the fulfillment of known requests.

Some wag will always say, "Well, if God knows everything that He's going to do, and if there is nothing that can stay His hand, what in the world is the purpose of our sitting down and taking time in prayer?" That is as a result of a misunderstanding of the way in which God works His purposes out, and it is a danger. Father knows best, but Scripture tells us our real power in this corrupt world is prayer. Christians need to remember God wants a relationship He equated to a marriage. According to Scripture, communicating with Father allows us to be part of His sovereign plans. He is sovereign, and Satan is not; therefore, we can use the mystery of spiritual prayer as our weapon in this world. If you can't wrap your mind around it, just believe it.

Vision Two: Fire

> This is what the Lord God showed me: behold, the Lord God was calling for a judgment by fire, and it devoured the great deep and was eating up the land. Then I said, "O Lord God, please cease! How can Jacob stand? He is so small!" The Lord relented concerning this: "This also shall not be," said the Lord God. (Amos 7:4–6 ESV)

Notice he didn't ask God to forgive them. He had asked that once, but God won't forgive unrepentant people. He won't apply forgiveness to an unchanged heart. Instead, this time he went straight to pleading for God's mercy. And what did God do? He showed mercy. Israel didn't ask for it. Israel hadn't repented.

Vision Three: The Plumb Line

The plumb line will not bend to culture, money, skin color, or a vote of democracy.

Time to Measure Up

In my first year of college, I found a part time job doing clean up labor on a major construction site. All I did was fetch and carry for the skilled workers building a housing complex. One time I carried lumber for a finishing carpenter who was struggling with pen and paper to figure square footage and lumber requirements. I looked at his problem and gave him the answer. He asked me, "You can do that in your head?"

"Yes," I said.

"You will spend the rest of the day with me," he proclaimed.

This skilled carpenter told the other men of my math abilities, and soon I was in demand all over the construction site. It wasn't long before management noticed the skilled labor was getting more done with less material waste, and I was given a substantial raise in wage. I learned the advantage of proper measurements and alignments. It was also the first time I saw a plumb line being used. A plumb line is a weighted piece of metal suspended on a cord. The force of gravity holds the string straight up from the center of the earth. Like lumber cut to mathematical principals, a plumb line insures something is built straight and upright.

> This is what he showed me: behold, the Lord was standing beside a wall built with a plumb line, with a plumb line in his hand. And the LORD said to me, "Amos, what do you see?" And I said, "A plumb line." Then the Lord said, "Behold, I am setting a plumb line in the midst of my people Israel; I will never again pass by them; the high places of Isaac shall be made desolate, and the sanctuaries of Israel shall be laid waste, and I will rise against the house of Jeroboam with the sword." (Amos 7:7–9 ESV)

Like math, the plumb line is not subjective. It is not based on personality, abilities, or sentiment. The plumb line will not bend to culture, money, skin color, or a vote of democracy. It is based in the composition of the universe and never subject to the whims of humanity. Isaiah 28:17 states:

> "And I will make justice the line, and righteousness the plumb line." (ESV)

God's purpose is stating Israel was built true to plumb, neither wonky nor out of kilter. He now wants to use the plumb line to measure how the nation currently stacks up. Israel is now out of alignment and needs to be torn down and rebuilt.

Take note of how quickly God impeded any appeal from Amos. He states that He will never again pass over Israel. The fact is, there comes a point when God will no longer listen to intercession. There seems to even be a point when God forbids intercession. At that mark, the intercessor becomes the chief witness against the sinners—a scary situation When does that happen? I don't know. Do you ever want to find out? As for Israel, the matter was settled; this vision would be fulfilled with no further delay.

Israel is a leaning wall in desperate need of correction. God appears to choose three targets for this judgment: first, the high places in Israel where local cult foreign gods were worshipped; second, the sanctuaries in Bethel and Dan, homes for the golden calf idols, cities that were also home to the phony priesthood; finally, the palaces of Jeroboam II, Israel's reigning king. In one fell swoop, God will collapse the social, religious, and political institutions that had propped up idolatry and injustice.

Ruth Graham is said to have told her husband Billy, "If God doesn't punish America, He'll have to apologize to Sodom and Gomorrah."

Final Thoughts

We've already explored social and biblical justice. What other institutions built to the Lord's standards are now tilted out of plumb in America? At judgment it will not matter whether my life plumbs straighter than yours. We will be compared to the perfect standard found in Christ, not against each other. He is the plumb line by which we must measure ourselves. Picture a vision of our corporate church and nation. How will they plumb?

Ruth Graham is said to have told her husband Billy, "If God doesn't punish America, He'll have to apologize to Sodom and Gomorrah."[31] On February 12, 2004, the first same sex marriage was performed in San Francisco, California. Del Martin and Phyllis Lyon became the first gay couple to receive official recognition as marriage.[32] From that moment a very sophisticated assault on God's biblical institution of the family has expanded to thirty-seven states legalizing same sex marriage. A plumb-lined institution established in the first book of the Bible is now askew.

What about the way we treat human beings? Who else but God could design the human body from earth materials? He created and vented into that physical body the breath of life. Have you ever thought of how the human body and the human soul cooperate? While we live in the body, we not only house the soul but also the body and soul have a vital connection. This is an amazing phenomenon. We create mechanical robots to perform certain types of work and AI computer programs. Yet man will never have the ability to create what God has created in the human—a soul possessing body, intellect, emotion, and will. Balance this idea with the abortion industry. Here are the most current figures I could find:

1. Total number of abortions in the U.S. 19732–019: 62.4 million+

2. 195 abortions per 1,000 live births (according to the Centers for Disease Control)

3. U.S. Abortions in 2017: ~862,320 (Guttmacher Institute)

4. Abortions per day: 2362+ (GI)

5. Abortions per hour: 98+ (GI)

6. 1 abortion every 37 seconds (GI)

7. 13.5 abortions / 1000 women aged 154–4 in 2017 (GI)[33]

On average, women give at least three reasons for choosing abortion: 3/4 say that having a baby would interfere with work, school, or other responsibilities; about 3/4 say they cannot afford a child; and 1/2 say they do not want to be a single parent or are having problems with their husband or partner.[34] I wonder at how many of these problems would have been mitigated if the American family unit had not been under attack all these years. And these are only American statistics. Another wonky plumbline.

The church does not need to be laser focused on social justice; but should be focused on God's justice. Under God's justice, our only hope is faith in Jesus where social problems would disappear.

Applications

1. Does God's discipline upon people who call His name, communicate their need for Him?

2. Amos pleaded for mercy and pronounced judgment. What does that tell us about God's prophets?

3. If someone says, "Preachers should stick only to the gospel," how would you respond?

Chapter Ten

Redneck Go Home

"The ultimate test of your greatness is the way you treat every human being."[35]
—Pope John Paul II

The Challenge

If you are paranoid, never go to Communist China in Christian service. I guarantee someone is watching you. In the same vein, if you have thin skin never become a church pastor. As pastor you sit in the center of the bullseye for controversy, inside and outside your congregation. There is a comfort bias for religious leaders to play it safe. We preachers are always tempted not to upset the apple cart and often must pick our battles to remain sane. There are always some people who will want to confront you frequently for some sermon comment or position you proclaim. An honest pastor praises the Lord for blessed congregational additions and a few blessed subtractions. I frequently reminded myself of Jesus' teaching: "If the world hates you, be aware that it hated me first" (see John 15:18). The good pastor knows that the price of peace may be too high a price to pay. Each ordained man has a charge that cannot be cheapened.

God set standards, and our modern world does not like them.

> "I charge you in the presence of God and of Christ Jesus, who is to judge the living and the dead, and by his appearing and his kingdom: preach the word; be ready in season and out of season; reprove, rebuke, and exhort, with complete patience and teaching" 2 Timothy 4:1–2 ESV)

When you stand up against what the Bible defines as sin, the world quickly forgets you also teach that all mankind are sinners with salvation easily accessed. We Christians are often called intolerant because we believe and proclaim the Bible. God set standards, and our modern world does not like them.

I believe the New Testament church is ministered through spiritual gifts. I'm a simple scholar and Bible teacher. Yet I've met evangelists who seem to enter a pulpit, sneeze a couple of times, and people get saved. I will sometimes, foolishly, look for a rational explanation. I wonder, "What in the world did he say to cause such a response?" Of course, we know Christ is the true evangelist, and only the Spirit saves. With confessed envy, I wish someone would say of me, "The land cannot bear all his words." One could claim success, like Amos, when you scare the politicians similar to Amaziah the priest. The intolerance of Amos the Prophet could not be tolerated by Amaziah priest of Bethel.

> Then Amaziah the priest of Bethel sent to Jeroboam king of Israel, saying, "Amos has conspired against you in the midst of the house of Israel. The land is not able to bear all his words. For thus Amos has said, 'Jeroboam shall die by the sword, and Israel must go into exile away from his land.'" (Amos 7:10–11 ESV)

Amaziah was the high priest of Bethel, one of the two state sanctuaries established by Jeroboam I. He broke away from Jerusalem to establish the Northern Kingdom in Samaria (see 1 Kings 12:26–33).

In order to unite the Northern ten tribes around his rule, Jeroboam I created a new shrine and a duplicate religious system. He established an alternative system with a calf idol, altar, priesthood, and festivals at Bethel to give credence and stability to the Northern Kingdom. In other words, it was an established political faith corrupted from the system handed down to Moses.

Amaziah, high priest of the false faith, creates a bogus charge to set before the king. Notice that Amaziah does not acknowledge God in the prophecies. He tells the king these were Amos's words. A phony preacher reduces Amos's challenges as coming from another phony preacher. They are so lost they cannot see God in the world anymore.

This politician does not reveal his own interest in the deportation of Amos. His seemingly patriotic concern is only for the welfare of Israel because "the land is not able to bear all his word." People were beginning to listen to the prophet, perhaps even daring to analyze conditions and speak of reform. Such action seemed like high treason to the priest of Bethel. Allowing Amos to continue his activity would endanger the welfare of the state. Amaziah chose to meet Amos as a threat to the status quo rather than as a messenger from God.

The Politician and the Prophet

In this recorded incident we get to see God's plumb line in operation to measure prophets and politicians. The vision had revealed that Israel's institutions, both religious and political, had failed the test and would have to come down. Now the sovereign Lord takes the measure of two men—one a prophet, the other a priest. One was accepted; the other was not. One obeyed the voice of the Lord; the other refused to hear.

> And Amaziah said to Amos, "O seer, go, flee away to the land of Judah, and eat bread there, and prophesy there, but never again prophesy at Bethel, for it is the king's sanctuary, and it is a temple of the kingdom." (7:12 ESV)

> *Stupidity apexed in the Netherlands where a Covid vaccination was required from anybody requesting euthanasia.*

One of the silliest things to come out of the Covid pandemic was coercing inoculations on the public, a shot that didn't even prevent the disease because of new variants. Stupidity apexed in the Netherlands where a Covid vaccination was required from anybody requesting euthanasia. The arrogance of Bethel's priest probably shook Amos to his core. Amaziah flirted with euthanasia, committing suicide by ignoring the God he was supposedly serving. He chose to serve the state instead of the creator.

In telling Amos to "eat bread" in Judah, Amaziah is claiming that Amos was a prophet for hire looking for a handout. He speaks to Amos like one con artist to another. Notice Amos was not about to toss testosterone or get in some sort of spiting contest. He would not trade insult for insult. Amaziah had heard the word of the Lord but rejected it, because it did not fit in with his own views or ideas. Also, he despised God's servant because he was not a professional clergyman.

Having dispatched his letter to the king, Amaziah then confronted Amos with the strong directive, "Get out, you seer!" Claiming authority over the activities at Bethel, the priest ordered Amos to go back to his home in Judah and do his prophesying there.

A *seer* (see Amos 7:12) was another name for a prophet (see 1 Samuel 9:9; 2 Samuel 24:11; Isaiah. 29:10) whose ministry came from visions. Amaziah, reacting to Amos's visions (see Amos 7:1, 4, 7), used the word in a derogatory sense. His scornful advice to earn your bread in Judah implied that Amos was a professional predictor who made his living selling prophecies. I once saw a Buddhist monk selling "lucky lottery numbers" on the streets of Bangkok. Next to his booth was a man selling lottery tickets. You get a taste of Amaziah's view of ministry from these words. He is like the televangelist giving out Peter and Paul salt and pepper shakers for a specified donation.

The stress in Amaziah's words fell on the location or geography of Amos's activity: "Go to Judah, earn your bread there, do your prophesying there, but don't prophesy anymore at Bethel." In his authority as the king's priest, he commanded Amos, "Leave Israel!" Amos's response, however, was that a greater authority commanded him to prophesy in Israel.

Why was the prophet from Tekoa unwelcomed? In denouncing Bethel and its system of worship, he attacked the very foundation of the kingdom. Bethel to Samaria had the same import as the temple in Jerusalem did for Judah. Bethel's shrine was the king's sanctuary and the temple. Besides being the site where Jeroboam II worshiped, it symbolically rallied political commitment to the kingdom. As the temple in Jerusalem drew devotion to the lineage of David, so the existence of Bethel implied God's sanctioned and supported the Northern monarch.

> Then Amos answered and said to Amaziah, "I was no prophet, nor a prophet's son, but I was a herdsman and a dresser of sycamore figs. But the LORD took me from following the flock, and the LORD said to me, 'Go, prophesy to my people Israel.'" (Amos 7:14 ESV)

Amos realized that he was nobody without God. He wasn't a prophet by birth. He didn't have the credentials. He hadn't been to the school of the prophets. He was a simple shepherd. Amos's birth didn't make him special. His name didn't make him special. His job didn't make him special. But His God did make him special. God called him. God gave him a message. And God sent him. All Amos had to do was obey Him. And he did. He confidently understood the source of his message, and he boldly proclaimed the strength of his message. The message is always greater than the messenger.

He had been profitably and contentedly occupied as a shepherd and as a grower of sycamore-fig trees. But one day the LORD "took" him—the same verb is used for God's calling the Levites in Numbers 18:6

and David in 2 Samuel 7:8—and told him exactly where to minister. God had commanded him not only what to say but also where to say it. The authority was not Amaziah's, but the Lord's. The place, therefore, would not be Judah, but Israel. The Lord had spoken, and Amos would prophesy as directed.

> Now therefore hear the word of the LORD. "You say, 'Do not prophesy against Israel, and do not preach against the house of Isaac.' Therefore, thus says the LORD: "'Your wife shall be a prostitute in the city, and your sons and your daughters shall fall by the sword, and your land shall be divided up with a measuring line; you yourself shall die in an unclean land, and Israel shall surely go into exile away from its land.'" (Amos 7:16–17 ESV)

Amaziah greeted Amos like a street prostitute defending her territory from competition. Had Amaziah responded differently, he might have been spared. Instead, he aligned with an earthly monarch and asserted his authority against God's messenger. So the Lord quietly withdrew the plumb line. He would spare Amaziah no longer. He and his family would suffer the full fate of the nation.

In denying the word of the Lord, his distinguished wife would end her life on streets of Samaria. His children will die in the conflict. His lands will be divided among the conqueror, and he, himself, will die in a pagan country. This message was very blunt. It was no longer a general call to all of Israel but a specific statement about the future of Amaziah and his family. The Lord's word would be fulfilled and Israel "will certainly go into exile, away from their native land."

Here is a truth that cannot be ignored—the infection of sin throughout the culture cannot occur without the permission of the people.

These are terrible things to befall anyone, but this scene highlights the folly of knowing God's word but failing to obey it. As high priest of one of the sanctuaries in Israel, he also failed in the responsibility of urging the people to obey the word of the Lord. Like King Saul in 1 Samuel 15:23, he "rejected the word of the Lord," so he himself was rejected as a servant of God.

Here is a truth that cannot be ignored—the infection of sin throughout the culture cannot occur without the permission of the people. If the people within a culture refuse to permit wickedness to reign unchecked in that society, the land will avoid the disastrous moral slide into the dissolution of character. However, whenever a culture allows wickedness to grow, that society will continue slipping away. History demonstrates God judges immoral nations.

Final Thoughts

When I entered my first pastoral office, I posted a photograph of Dietrich Bonhoeffer. Pastor Bonhoeffer stayed in Nazi Germany to challenge the state church and government into following the teaching of Christ. Bonhoeffer was murdered on order of Adolf Hitler in the last days of World War II. I transferred that picture to every ministry office I ever inhabited. It attempted to remind me to keep a backbone for Jesus, no matter the consequences. In China I associated with a man of God I will name as Pastor Hu. That is not his real name for security reasons. *Hu* simply means *tiger* in Mandarin and reflected his personality. Pastor Hu was baptizing seventy-five to three hundred new believers every month in the years I knew him. Yet he had been arrested and communistically re-educated a total of five times. He is still Spirit-fired with the gospel. I wish many of our church leaders in America would grow a backbone and stand for the plumb line of Scripture. I know of no church in this country that baptize seventy-five to three hundred new believers every month.

The church in America should take some responsibility for the despicable moral condition of our nation. We have kept our mouths shut; we've minded our own business and quietly tolerated all of these things. As a result, many American churches are on life support, and the church is in danger of experiencing the discipline and judgment of the Lord, just as Israel did.

Do you know politically incorrect people? To be politically incorrect means that you say things and do things that wouldn't go over very well politically. The media would disagree with you. Lots of people would say that you are intolerant, unkind, or narrow-minded. To be politically incorrect means that you don't agree with the popular opinions of the day. If you follow Jesus Christ, then you also are politically incorrect. His Word teaches what is moral and what is immoral. A very different idea from what the world around you believes. If you are a follower of Jesus Christ, then, whether you like it or not, you are politically incorrect.

The Bible is not a self-help book to make our lives on earth easy and comfortable. The Bible isn't written to give us the steps to overcoming worry or to teach us how to manage our finances or be successful in our work or to conquer your fears, although God does provide answers to all these life problems. The Bible is written primarily to reveal the character of God and call for us to return to Him and live for Him.

Maybe we Christians need a reminder of the consequences history teaches us about being politically incorrect. Luke was hanged upon an olive tree in the classic land of Greece. John was put in a cauldron of boiling oil, but escaped in a miraculous manner and was afterward banished to Patmos. Peter was crucified at Rome with his head downward. James, the son of Zebedee, was beheaded at Jerusalem. James, the son of Alphaeus, was thrown from a lofty pinnacle of the temple, and then beaten to death with a fuller's club. Bartholomew was flayed alive. Andrew was bound to a cross from which he preached to his persecutors until he died. Thomas was run through the body with a lance at Coromandel in the East Indies. Jude was shot to death with arrows.

Matthias was first stoned and then beheaded. Barnabas of the Gentiles was stoned to death at Salonika. Paul, after various tortures and persecutions, was beheaded at Rome by the Emperor Nero. God is not for "spare tire" use as some product for our comfort. We are here for His glory and service.

Application

1. Read Job 5:7; 1 Thessalonians 3:4; 1 Peter 4:12–19. What do these verses teach us about the testing of faith in the Christian's life?

2. What were the causes for opposition to Amos?

3. Why would there be opposition to Bible teaching from religious leaders? Why is the issue of authority important?

4. How can a Christian politician remain true to the Word of God? (Psalms. 139:12–24; Amos 5:14; Romans 2:6–11; Ephesians 4:15.)

5. Can a person be called into the work of the gospel without going to Bible college? How can we decide whether a person is called into such work or not?

Chapter Eleven

The Time is Ripe

*"We can never be gods, but we can become something
less than human with frightening ease.*[36]
—NK Jemisin

Basket of Fruit and Israel's Captivity

To the chagrin of my beautiful wife, I love puns. God, too, used a dead pan sense of humor for a grave subject. He entombed a pun about the dead buried in the picture of a basket of ripe fruit. He buried a pun in the vision in a harvest of summer produce. In a fruitful use of Hebrew idioms, Amos entombed the word used for *summer fruit* with a sound alike word used for the *end*. Unfortunately, this bountiful fruiting image terminates the yields in a harvest of corpses.

The emphasis of the ripe fruit image means the finality judgment is conclusive.

This is what the Lord God showed me, and, and behold, there was there was a basket of summer fruit. And He said, "What do you see, Amos?" And I said, "A basket of summer fruit." Then the Lord said to me, ""The end has come for My people Israel. I will not spare them any longer. The songs of the palace will turn to wailing on that day," declares the Lord GOD. "The corpses will be many; in every place they will throw them out. Hush!" (Amos 8:1–3 NASB)

The emphasis of the ripe fruit image means the finality judgment is conclusive. The basket of ripe fruit symbolizes a completed harvest. In identifying "summer fruit," he declares the end of the agricultural season. God acceded twice to Amos's intersession, but this image says, "Time is up!" The sanctuary worship songs will become lamentations. Dead bodies will pile up where there are too many to bury. So innumerable will be the slaughter, the people will lift wet questioning eyes toward heaven. They only find the sounds of silence. The songs mentioned were the celebration of a good harvest. Now they turned instead to wailing cries. Still God identifies them as "my people Israel," a phrase used with the plumb line Amos 7:8 as well as the confrontation with Amaziah in Amos 7:15, the point being, God still recognizes His covenant relationship and will use the national judgments as a purging instead of extermination.

Never on Sunday

The people's greed generated an unjust and dishonest society.

I'm old enough to remember when stores were closed on Sundays in order to give employees a day of rest. This cultural concept changed sometime in the 1970s when profit margins became more important than employees. At the same period, family businesses converted to corporations to avoid moral implications and law suits. Personal ethics gave way to pragmatics of lawyers, and our nation has spiraled morally down since.

The web site called *The Macro Elephant* wrote,
"Greed is a powerful force that becomes a corrupting influence on people and their environment as money is seen to equal power and as the wealthy are seen to have more power, they assume that it becomes their right to have more authority over those people in the community that have a lot less. This creates a separation in the different socio-economic classes, which leads to inequality which in turn propagates more greed. Corruption evolves when those who have higher authority are able to abuse their power, causing chaos as more of the population become victims of crimes that impact their financial well-being. Businesses riddled with payment scandals, government officials perverting the disbursement of taxpayer dollars and burdening economies with excessive debts, individuals gouging businesses and the public purse in the pursuit of more money and assets are ever increasing."[37]

Amos Chapter 8, at this point, circles back to the similar setting in Israel, back to one of the major themes of the book. Specifically, the people's greed generated an unjust and dishonest society.

> Hear this, you who trample the needy, to put an end to the humble of the land, saying, "When will the new moon be over, so that we may sell grain; And the Sabbath, so that we may open the wheat market, to make the ephah smaller and the shekel bigger, And to cheat with dishonest scales, so as to buy the helpless for money, And the needy for a pair of sandals, and that we may sell the refuse of the wheat?" (Amos 8:4–6 NASB)

In using the word *trample*, Amos vividly paints barbaric treatment of vulnerable citizens. He explicitly says that the elite class devours the humble. These are the offenders God is charging with iniquity. The elements of the crimes are illustrated from quoting their own words.

These merchants were exasperated when worship interfered with commerce. Annoyed with Sabbath shut downs, they dreamed of cheating their customers while participating in services. Four different methods of cheating their customers are mentioned. The use of different weights was specifically prohibited in Mosaic law. An ephah was a volume measure for grain at about eight gallons. By shrinking the size of the measurement container, the merchant stretched his product sales and increased profits. The shekel was a unit of weight secretly enhanced to make the customer put more silver to balance. The third cheat rigged the scales to gain advantage with corrupt measures. A fourth cheat is mentioned at adding chaff to inferior grain only to sell to the poor.

These unethical merchants perverted justice further by quickly taking the cheated insolvent poor into servitude for small debts, selling whole families to further profits.

Shake Rattle and Roll

> The LORD has sworn by the pride of Jacob, "Indeed, I will never forget any of their deeds. Because of this will the land not quake, and everyone who lives in it mourn? Indeed, all of it will rise up like the Nile, and it will be tossed about and subside like the Nile of Egypt. And it will come about on that day," declares the Lord GOD, "That I will make the sun go down at noon, and make the earth dark in broad daylight. (Amos 8:7–9 NASB)

This is probably the earthquake mentioned in chapter one where the land rolled up and subsided like annual flooding of the Nile. Palestinian solar eclipses were visible in 784 BC and 763 BC.

People say time heals all wounds. God is saying in these verses that mourning over the death will be like the first day it happened.

Then I will turn your festivals into mourning, and all your songs into songs of mourning; And I will put sackcloth around everyone's waist, and baldness on every head. And I will make it like a time of mourning for an only son, the end of it will be like a bitter day. (Amos 8:10 NASB)

People say time heals all wounds. God is saying, in these verses, that mourning over the death will be like the first day it happened. Everyone will feel the impact of mourning like a family with only one child mourning his death. The judgment is that they will feel the full impact of the death every day. Time will not lessen the hurt.

We began this chapter as God gave Amos a basket of ripe fruit. It represented the people of Israel, because they were ripe or ready for punishment. Next merchants kept religious festivals, impatient for services to end. When holy days and Sabbaths concluded, they could go back to making money. Bettering themselves was life's objective, even if it meant cheating others. Their heart was not in worship; it was on themselves. A religious front was good business, but God knew their hearts. He was not pleased. What should He do with people who have no appetite for His Word? His answer was simple; take His voice away from unbelievers.

A Biblical Famine

In 1968 the USS Pueblo,[38] a navy intelligence ship, was boarded and captured by North Korea. The crew was held captive for eleven months in a country where it was a death sentence to possess a copy of the Bible. These tortured and beaten prisoners created what they called the "Pueblo Bible" where each man would recall portions of Scripture they had memorized. These men held to tiny pieces of the Word of God for comfort. If the Bible was taken from us, how many would really miss it?

From a survey released March 17, 2022, George Barna found only forty percent of American parents considered the Bible to be "God's accurate word for humanity." Another disturbing statistic from this survey of parents was their world view. Two thirds or sixty-seven percent identified themselves as Christian Americans. This is consistent with other survey data. Yet, of this sixty-seven percent only two percent subscribed to a world view identified as "accepting the Bible as a relevant and authoritative guide for life."[39] A famine is a lack of nutrition. Losing the Bible would be a lack of ethical, moral, and spiritual nutrition. Famine is a time of great deprivation—starvation, want, poverty, deficiency, scarcity, and probably death. Anytime you hear the word *famine*, you should know things are out of shape and demand urgency.

Since Israel rejected God's Word, they don't have to hear it anymore.

> "Behold, days are coming," declares the Lord GOD, "When I will send a famine on the land, not a famine of bread or a thirst for water, but rather for hearing the words of the LORD. People will stagger from sea to sea and from the north even to the east; They will roam about to seek the word of the LORD, but they will not find it. On that day the beautiful virgins and the young men will faint from thirst.
>
> As for those who swear by the guilt of Samaria, and say, 'As your god lives, Dan,' And, 'As the way of Beersheba lives,' They will fall and not rise again." (Amos 8:11–14 NASB)

Since Israel rejected God's word, they don't have to hear it anymore, a famine of biblical ignorance pronounced by the sovereign Lord himself. Men would stagger to every corner of the land, wandering in a complete circuit of Israel's territory searching for the word of the Lord. But they would not find it. Even the strongest and youngest will exhaust themselves searching. In the vacuum, those pushing the political pagan alternatives will come to final judgment.

Not Nirvana

Nirvana is defined as a place of perfect peace and happiness, like heaven. In Hinduism and Buddhism *nirvana* is the highest state someone can attain, a state of enlightenment, meaning a person's individual desires and suffering go away.

> I saw the LORD standing beside the altar, and He said, "Strike the pillar capitals so that the thresholds will shake, and break them on the heads of them all! Then I will put to death the rest of them with the sword; They will not have a fugitive who will flee, nor a survivor who will escape. Though they dig into Sheol, from there My hand will take them; And though they ascend to heaven, from there I will bring them down. And though they hide on the summit of Carmel, I will track them down and take them from there; And though they hide themselves from My sight on the bottom of the sea, I will command the serpent from there, and it will bite them. And though they go into captivity before their enemies, from there I will command the sword and it will kill them, And I will set My eyes against them for harm and not for good." (Amos 9:1–4 NASB)

In agrarian Israel, the autumn harvest festival had the congregation assembling at Bethel's sanctuary with the king in attendance. The people expected their king to stand by the altar for a harvest blessing. Amos pictures the people finding the Lord, himself standing by the altar. Unfortunately for Israel no blessing was forthcoming, only judgment.

This vision summarizes the things promised in previous visions. This time no hope of reconciliation is offered, only death.

Here the Lord himself gives two commands. First strike the ceilings, then make sure roof falls on everyone's head. Second, the blood-curdling command is to cut the heads off all the survivors. The Lord is adamant no one should escape, the point being, no one may hide from the wrath of God.

The Impartial Sovereign

> The Lord GOD of armies, The One who touches the land so that it quakes, And all those who live in it mourn, and all of it rises up like the Nile and subsides like the Nile of Egypt; The One who builds His upper chambers in the heavens and has founded His vaulted dome over the earth, He who calls for the waters of the sea and pours them out on the face of the earth, The LORD is His name. (Amos 9:5–6 NIV)

Amos 9:7 is probably the most important piece of theology in the book of Amos.

Every Nations Sovereign God

Amos 9:7 is probably the most important piece of theology in the book of Amos. Unfortunately, the spiritual meaning is lost in time and culture, yet it is crucial for us Gentiles.

> "Are you not as the sons of Ethiopia to Me, You sons of Israel?" declares the LORD. "Have I not brought up Israel from the land of Egypt, And the Philistines from Caphtor and the Arameans from Kir?" (Amos 9:7 NASB)

Israel's special position as His people would not save them from punishment, although many placed their confidence in being the chosen people. God is the Sovereign of every nation. God would act toward them as toward any other nation within His universal domain. He had not only brought Israel out of Egypt; He also guided their enemies—the Philistines from Caphtor and the Arameans from Kir. The thought Amos had nothing to do with all fallen descendants of Adam and everything only to do the Israelites is misguided. Prophets like Amos had the habit of talking about New Testament spiritual realities using Old Testament pictures. Here he is saying Yahweh could have used the pagans next door just as easy as the Hebrews. Every human is subject to his sovereignty.

Final Thoughts

Biblical illiteracy is the current danger facing our own culture. When we want guidance, do we consider what God has to say or consult the Guru of the Month Club? Scripture is a lamp to our feet, a light for our path. The world will either stumble in the dark or walk in the light.

Can you imagine what the world would be like if there was a spiritual famine? If there were people who were searching for the Word and could not find it. I imagine overflowing prisons because of no repentance. I imagine uncontrolled homelessness because no one helps the poor, mentally ill, or the addicted without Christians. How about rampant growth of STDs without the moral precepts of marriage. Maybe parents will kill children, children will kill parents, children will kill children and abandoned children because family is no longer a priority. Since marriage has no more meaning, such a society would have males marrying males and females marrying females. Without family values, males and females could just live together without marriage. Think of the crime in a spiritual famine—hate crimes, terrorist attacks, extensive theft, and proliferating brutality. Forget social justice, because justice doesn't exist without an external plumb line. Without a moral compass, people will have nothing to repent; therefore, selfishness rules, and survival of the strongest becomes the law. Morality of the barnyard becomes society's norm. It would be frightening to live in such a society without Jesus Christ. Think of all the promises God has given us through his Son. God promised to provide our daily clothes and food. He promised to protect us and to work everything for our good. He promised strength in the midst of trial. He has promised eternal life.

Application

1. Read Leviticus 25. How does God want His people treated compared to foreigners? Why the difference?

2. Compare and contrast the sins delineated in Amos 8:4–6 with Amos 2:6–8.

3. Does the peril in Amos 8:10 extend to any wicked nation? Is such a nation left to their own resources?

4. What events in current culture seem strikingly familiar with the events of Amos 8?

Chapter Twelve

A Way Forward

*"Love and compassion are necessities, not luxuries.
Without them, humanity cannot survive."*[40]
—Dali Lama XIV

"It is a terrifying thing to fall into the hands of the living God."
—Hebrews 10:31 (NASB)

The impetus of Scripture now changes from destruction to discipline. The process of purification must continue, yet once again God's wrath is mitigated with hope to those who will still honor Him. God always wants to correct not consume. God choose the Hebrew people to demonstrate righteousness, mercy, and justice to the pagan world. When His people fail in His purposes, then they are no longer blessed above the rest of creation. He will treat all sinners with equality. Israel's faith deteriorated until God was little more than a cult deity. If they chose to act like pagans, they received the same treatment as the pagans. In final chapter of Amos, we again view the doctrine of the remnant. When God punishes groups and nations, a small portion survive because they have stood against the popular grain. Think about Noah's family from the flood or Lot at Sodom and Gomorrah. Again, only Josuha and Caleb were allowed to enter the promised land of Canaan. In our own future, this doctrine is proclaimed in the book of Revelations.

---

*Established forms of religion prosper,
but many are a veneer covering hypocrisy and avarice.*

"Behold, the eyes of the Lord God are on the sinful kingdom, And I will destroy it from the face of the earth; Nevertheless, I will not totally destroy the house of Jacob," Declares the Lord. (Amos 9:8 NASB)

My early science background provides a plethora of illustrations for scriptural concepts. The Granny Smith apple is one of Australia's greatest agricultural achievements. Maria Anne Smith of New South Wales composted a pile of rotten crab apples, which sprouted a sapling. From discarded spoiled remains, a new breed of apple captured a billion-dollar industry. God can create wonderful things from something decimated and cast away. Thus, the doctrine of the remnant is an important biblical concept.

Amos preached his message to the ancient Israelites, yet if we ignore changes in technology, history, and circumstances, the fundamentals of his society permeate our own culture. Corruption, cruelty, and injustice remain fixed in the public square. Established forms of religion prosper, but many are a veneer covering hypocrisy and avarice. History shows when God's tolerance comes to an end, the entire construct must be destroyed to let the remnant thrive.

The ninth chapter of Amos highlights a New Testament picture of our God. He demands righteous living while offering a path of redemption. He will not accept second place status in our lives nor second place discipleship. There will be accounting, not only after death, but every day we live. The judgments and punishments are never an end in themselves. Vengeance is not the objective; always He seeks reconciliation. So naturally, He follows judgment with promised new beginnings.

> "For behold, I am commanding, And I will shake the house of Israel among all nations as grain is shaken in a sieve, but not a kernel will fall to the ground. "All the sinners of My people will die by the sword, those who say, 'The calamity will not overtake or confront us.'" (Amos 9:9–10 NASB)

Having declared that He would make no distinction between Israel and other nations, God then solemnly uttered His final statements of judgment in the Book of Amos—death vows are impartial and certain death to all the sinners of the land with no refuge from God except the refuge that is found in God.

God chose the Hebrew people to be not only a nation themselves but as moral examples to the rest of the world. His people among all the nations will also be sifted for integrity. The grain sieve is an easy illustration to understand. Filtering out the chaff and dust catching only the valuable wheat kernels visualizes God screening to save any righteous among His people. This is similar to using an impartial plumb line separating the righteous from the sinners.

Restoration of David

> "In that day I will raise up the fallen booth of David, and wall up its breaches; I will also raise up its ruins and rebuild it as in the days of old; That they may possess the remnant of Edom and all the nations who are called by My name," Declares the LORD who does this. (Amos 9:11–12 NASB)

The collapsed "booth of David" was a shelter for the people under a righteous king. Amos is saying David's rule had crumbled, but God will rebuild restoring David's greatness. The promise of the house of David ruling over the nations of earth is not a new prophecy with Amos. The reader should investigate Psalm 2 and Psalm 72. Yet Amos was the first prophet to link this resurrection of Davidic reign to the "day of the Lord." The fulfillment of many of these prophecies came at the incarnation of Jesus Christ and future blessing at His second coming.

We may look at our world and feel something similar to collapsed righteousness. It is a situation where God always had a plan. Read Jeremiah 31:31–34:

> "Behold, days are coming," declares the Lord, "when I will make a new covenant with the house of Israel and the house of Judah, not like the covenant which I made with their fathers in the day I took them by the hand to bring them out of the land of Egypt, My covenant which they broke, although I was a husband to them," declares the Lord. "For this is the covenant which I will make with the house of Israel after those days," declares the Lord: "I will put My law within them and write it on their heart; and I will be their God, and they shall be My people. They will not teach again, each one his neighbor and each one his brother, saying, 'Know the Lord,' for they will all know Me, from the least of them to the greatest of them," declares the Lord, "for I will forgive their wrongdoing, and their sin I will no longer remember." (NASB)

Jeremiah puts into words the sworn ending of an Old Testament theme with the New Testament beginning. The promises made to Abraham are only partially fulfilled because the people of God continued to be disobedient. After the death of Solomon, civil war splits the Hebrews apart: Israel in the northern kingdom, Judah in the south. After two hundred years of separate existence, Israel itself morally implodes and Assyrians dismantled the partial kingdom. And in that period of time, the story of the kingdom is a story that is then prophesied. The Southern Kingdom hangs on for another century, and then it's destroyed and exiled into Babylon. The prophets are essentially coming to them and saying, "Come on now. You're supposed to be God's people, living in God's place, under God's rule, and enjoying God's blessing. Get on with it!" Amos renewed awareness of the cost of being chosen. The New Testament says we have been called to be saints, God's holy people, and appointed to live holy, righteous lives.

Amos earlier prophesied the sovereignty of God, accented to seek out those who might try to escape His judgment (see Amos 9:14). Now Amos calls on the sovereignty of God to seek out those whom He wanted to preserve. One of the most fascinating elements of the Christian faith is the characteristic of God to rebuild the broken.

A third-century skeptic named Celsus demeaned our faith to the Roman public with the following words: "When most teachers go forth to teach, they cry, 'Come to me, you who are clean and worthy,' and they are followed by the highest caliber of people available. But your silly master cries, 'Come to me, you who are down and beaten by life,' and so he accumulates around him the rag, tag and bobtail of humanity."[41]

The benefits of the gospel of Jesus Christ may draw people towards Christ but should not be taught as the reason to become a believer.

Origen, an early church father, replied: "Yes, they are the rag, tag and bobtail of humanity. But Jesus does not leave them that way. Out of material you would have thrown away as useless, he fashions men, giving them back their self-respect, enabling them to stand on their feet and look God in the eyes. They were cowed, cringing, broken things. But the Son has set them free."[42]

This is a great blessing in Christianity, but it is not the gospel and should never be presented as the gospel. The benefits of the gospel of Jesus Christ may draw people towards Christ but should not be taught as the reason to become a believer. Otherwise, we slide down the slope Amos condemns as Israel's false faith. God wants a relationship and worship, not the image of some Santa Claus in the sky. The gospel echoes an Old Testament theme, specifically a full trust in our creator God. We all have sinned against our creator and have only hope in His forgiveness. The difference is Jesus leaves His spirit to write the law on our inner being as Jeremiah stated. Jesus' advent means restoration. No, He hasn't come to fix up our houses; He came to restore the fallen "booth" of David and the fallen descendants of Adam.

> "The Son of Man came to seek and to save the lost." (Luke 19:10 NIV)

Extending David's Kingship

> That they may possess the remnant of Edom and all the nations who are called by My name," Declares the LORD who does this. "Behold, days are coming," declares the LORD, "When the plowman will overtake the reaper and the treader of grapes him who sows seed; When the mountains will drip sweet wine And all the hills will be dissolved." "Also, I will restore the captivity of My people Israel, and they will rebuild the ruined cities and live in them; They will also plant vineyards and drink their wine, And make gardens and eat their fruit. "I will also plant them on their land, and they will not again be rooted out from their land Which I have given them," says the LORD your God. (Amos 9:12–15 NASB)

Why does God say that the house of David will possess the remnant of Edom, when Obadiah 1:8 clearly affirms in "that day" Edom will be utterly destroyed? There is a remnant of Edom that will also flee to Mount Zion for deliverance as with Israel. If we use the Bible to interpret the Bible, James uses this verse as evidence the Gentiles must be accepted into the Christian church (see Acts 15:16–17). David's kingdom expands as the Christian church takes the gospel of Jesus Christ to all nations and tongues. Abraham had been promised that he would be the father of "many nations" (see Genesis 17:4), and these nations would include Gentile as well as Jewish peoples. Salvation is by grace alone through faith alone as soon as a sinner recognizes their enmity with God and their need for a savior. From the beginning, God's plan has been to provide salvation for the Gentile nations. His promise to Abraham was that through his descendants "all peoples on earth" will be blessed. Isaiah affirms the Messiah will bring light, justice, and full knowledge of the LORD to all nations on the earth. With Israel restored, the land will be so productive that the plowman and reaper are working at the same time. God promises the people will never be removed again.

Faith shapes people; people shape culture; culture shapes nations.

Final Thoughts

Common sense communicates we are trekking through an age of conflict. Satan is ramping up events seeking to usurp God's place, possibly bringing history to climax. The fight for the hearts and souls of humanity sees the polarization of two competing faiths. One is bogus; one is real. Like in the book of Amos, discerning the real faith comes from evaluating biblical justice in the followers of each group. We walk with people claiming to be Christians more influenced by Netflix than the Bible; they are evangelizing essential oils before Jesus Christ. Are warning signs again being broadcast in our times?

Faith shapes people; people shape culture; culture shapes nations. God needs to shape us. Problems are overwhelming our society: One black man choked to death by a policeman, two policemen shot dead in their patrol car. Drug abuse has a viselike grip. Materialism holds options and no answers. Politicians claim the answer lies in education or in wealth redistribution. And even a modicum of historical analysis is able to tell you that has never fixed anything before. It certainly can't fix a warped heart and life. A check engine light may annoy a vehicle owner, especially when it stays lit. The light can be ignored, but eventually a break down will occur. These are cured when the mechanic pulls the error code and reads the problem from the code book. We have a book to fix social errors.

Application

1. How did Amos destroy the concept that Israel would always have preferential treatment as the chosen people?

2. Read the following passages: Isaiah 27, 42–44, 65–66; Obadiah 17, 21; Jeremiah 30–33; Micah 7:14–20; Ezekiel 36–48; Zephaniah 3:14–20; Daniel 9:20–27; 12:1–3; Hagai 2:20–23; Hosea 2:14–23; 14:4–7, Joel 3:16–21; Malachi 4:1–3. What is the recurring theme?

3. Why is God's covenant with David important to Israel?

4. What did Amos consider as the result of the nation's being blessed?

5. What do you draw from the conclusion of the book of Amos?

6. What personal lessons has Amos revealed to you?

Endnotes

1 https://theartofliving.com/quote/we-can-know-only-that-leo-tolstoy/

2 *Cambridge Dictionary.* https://dictionary.cambridge.org/us/dictionary/english/redneck,

3 https://quotefancy.com/quote/1182424/Paul-Farmer-The-idea-that-some-lives-matter-less-is-the-root-of-all-that-is-wrong-with

4 Julian Resendiz, "Body Count from Drug Cartel Wars Earns Mexican Cities Lael of 'Most Violent in the World,'" BorderReport, https://www.borderreport.com/hot-topics/border-crime/body-count-from-drug-cartel-wars-earns-mexican-cities-label-of-most-violent-in-the-world/.

5 Walk Free Foundation https://www.ons.gov.uk/peoplepopulationandcommunity/crimeandjustice/articles/modernslaveryintheuk/march2020

6 https://www.globalslaveryindex.org/2018/findings/country-studies/united-kingdom/

7 [chapter 3] Universal Declaration of Human Rights, United Nations General Assembly in Paris on 10 December 1948 (General Assembly resolution 217 A) https://www.un.org/en/about-us/universal-declaration-of-human-rights

8 https://www.goodreads.com/quotes/215622-let-us-try-to-teach-generosity-and-altruism-because-we

9   ttp://www.quotss.com/quote/There-is-always-more-misery-among-the-lower-classes-than-there-is-humanity

10 https://www.goodreads.com/quotes/967627-the-quest-for-riches-darkens-the-sense-of-right-and

11 "All About BSE (Mad Cow Disease)," FDA, https://www.fda.gov/animal-veterinary/animal-health-literacy/all-about-bse-mad-cow-disease.

12 https://seattleatheist.church/faq/

13 https://www.goodreads.com/quotes/3140-a-single-death-is-a-tragedy-a-million-deaths-is

14 Adam Hartley, "Bloomberg publishes Steve Jobs' obituary" By published August 28, 2008 Senior News Editor for TechRadar.com https://www.techradar.com/in/news/computing/apple/bloomberg-publishes-steve-jobs-obituary-460848

15 Flew, Antony, and Gary R. Habermas, 2005, "My Pilgrimage from Atheism to Theism: An Exclusive Interview with Former British Atheist Professor Antony Flew," Philosophia Christi, Winter, http://www.biola.edu/antonyflew/flew-interview.pdf.

16. "Saving Jeffrey Dahmer," https://www.beliefnet.com/faiths/christianity/2006/11/saving-jeffrey-dahmer.aspx.

17 https://www.goodreads.com/quotes/7102175-all-that-is-necessary-for-evil-to-succeed-is-that

18 https://www.goodreads.com/quotes/341720-before-you-attempt-to-beat-the-odds-be-sure-you

19 C.S. Lewis, *Mere Christianity,* Digital Edition March 2021 page 52, HarperCollins Publishers Inc., 195 Broadway, New York, NY 10007 www.harpercollins.com

20 https://www.psychologytoday.com/us/blog/the-art-thinking-clearly/201306/the-overconfidence-effect

21 Sara Bauer, *The Restoration Attempts on Sea Otter Habitat after the Exxon Valdez Oil Spill in Prince William Sound*, The Restoration and Reclamation Review. Vol. 7, No. 3, Fall 2001

22 Martin Luther King Jr. (1929–1968) "I've Been to the Mountaintop" Memphis, Tennessee–April 3, 1968, https://www.afscme.org/about/history/mlk/mountaintop

23 https://kidadl.com/quotes/best-ever-john-bunyan-quotes-from-the-author-of-the-pilgrims-progress

24 https://www.goodreads.com/quotes/359784-hypocrite-the-man-who-murdered-his-parents-and-then-pleaded

25 https://www.dictionary.com/browse/humbug

26 https://deadorkicking.com/death-statistics/worldwide/2020/27.

27 https://reason.com/2009/01/07/the-death-of-one-man-is-a-trag/27.

28 https://www.goodreads.com/quotes/1256891-social-justice-cannot-be-attained-by-violence-violence-kills-what

29 Kevin Gaiss, *War in Ukraine to impact grain, food prices*, Mar. 10, 2022. https://www.wcax.com/2022/03/10/war-ukraine-impact-grain-food-prices/

30 Emma Charlton. *Locusts are putting 5 million people at risk of starvation – and that's without COVID-19*, 26 Jun 2020. https://www.weforum.org/agenda/2020/06/locusts-africa-hunger-famine-covid-19/

31 https://www.tldm.org/News26/if-god-doesnt-punish-america-hell-have-to-apologize-to-sodom-and-gomorrah.htm

32 "Same Sex Marriage States 2022", https://worldpopulationreview.com/state-rankings/same-sex-marriage-states.

33 https://www.all.org/abortion/abortion-statistics

34 Lawrence B. Finer Lori F. Frohwirth,Guttmacher Institute Lindsay A. Dauphinee Susheela Singh,Guttmacher Institute

Ann M. Moore, Guttmacher Institute. *Reasons U.S. Women Have Abortions: Quantitative and Qualitative Perspectives,* September 1, 2005. https://www.guttmacher.org/journals/psrh/2005/reasons-us-women-have-abortions-quantitative-and-qualitative-perspectives

35 https://quotefancy.com/quote/891202/Pope-John-Paul-II-The-ultimate-test-of-your-greatness-is-the-way-you-treat-every-human

36 https://quotefancy.com/quote/39900/N-K-Jemisin-We-can-never-be-gods-after-all-but-we-can-become-something-less-than-human

37 *Greed & Corruption – Business, Individuals & Government,* The Macro Elephant https://www.macroelephant.com/greed-corruption-business-individuals-government/

38 Julie A. Cohick, "The Pueblo Bible, December 1, 2016, https://wordoftruthlighthouse.blogspot.com/2016/12/pueblo-bible.html

39 https://www.worthynews.com/66746-poll-majority-of-us-parents-do-not-believe-bible-is-gods-word-shockingly-few-share-biblical-worldview-with-children?utm_source=wnd&utm_medium=wnd&utm_campaign=syndicated

40 https://www.goodreads.com/quotes/33159-love-and-compassion-are-necessities-not-luxuries-without-them-humanity

41 Jeff Strite, *Stewardship of a "Patchless" Life,* 1/3/2010, https://www.sermoncentral.com/sermon-illustrations/75194/redeeming-the-rag-tag-and-bobtail-by-sermon-central

42 Jeff Strite, *Stewardship of a "Patchless" Life,* 1/3/2010, https://www.sermoncentral.com/sermon-illustrations/75194/redeeming-the-rag-tag-and-bobtail-by-sermon-central